Composers of North America

Series Editors: Sam Dennison, William C. Loring, Margery Lowens, Ezra Schabas

No. 1 *William Wallace Gilchrist*, by Martha Furman Schleifer

No. 2 *Energy and Individuality in the Art of Anna Huntington, Sculptor, and Amy Beach, Composer*, by Myrna G. Eden

No. 3 *A Musical American Romantic Abroad: Templeton Strong and His Music*, by William C. Loring

William Wallace Gilchrist (1846-1916)

A Moving Force in the
Musical Life of Philadelphia

by
Martha Furman Schleifer

Composers of North America, No. 1

The Scarecrow Press, Inc.
Metuchen, N.J., and London
1985

Grateful acknowledgment is made to the following publishers
for permission to reprint brief musical examples and incipits:

Theodore Presser Co., and subsidiaries--

   John Church Co.
   Oliver Ditson Co.

927.8
G 467s

The Swedenborgian Church, including--

   New Church Press
   Swedenborg Publishing Association
   Swedenborg Press
   New Church Board of Publication
   General Convention of the New Jerusalem

General Church of the New Jerusalem

Belwin Mills Publishing Corp.

G. Schirmer, Inc.

87-925

Library of Congress Cataloging in Publication Data

Schleifer, Martha Furman.
 William Wallace Gilchrist, 1846-1916.

 (Composers of North America ; no. 1)
 Bibliography: p.
 Includes index.
 1. Gilchrist, William Wallace, 1846-1916.
2. Composers--United States--Biography. I. Title.
II. Series.
ML410.G353S3 1985 780'.92'4 [B] 84-27717
ISBN 0-8108-1784-5

CONTENTS

Foreword   v
Preface   vii
Acknowledgments   xi

I	The First Forty Years	1
II	European Tour--1886	11
III	1888-1916	15
IV	In Memoriam	26
V	The Mendelssohn Club	32
VI	The Manuscript Music Society	44
VII	Gilchrist's Music	51

Epilogue   67
Catalog   69
Index of First Lines   191
Sources Consulted   198

Index   205

This series is designed to restore an almost forgotten part of our musical heritage. Few North American composers had their works performed frequently enough during their lifetimes to establish them in the standard repertoire of soloists, chamber groups, orchestras, or choruses; their compositions, therefore, even when published, have tended to be forgotten.

Each volume begins with the life and works of a given composer, placing that person in the context of the musical world of the period and providing comments by contemporary critics. The authors note those compositions that today's listeners might enjoy. Each volume includes a catalog of the composer's works, complete with incipits, publication details, and locations of unpublished works.

The series will have served its purpose if it draws attention to the large body of work that has so long been treated with benign neglect. The editors believe that a number of these compositions are worthy of being performed today. They hope that those so indicated in text or catalog will be considered for performance by designers and conductors of concert programs and that performers will add some of these works to their repertoires.

> Sam Dennison, Margery M. Lowens, William C. Loring, J. Ezra Schabas, Series Editors

It is entirely appropriate that this series on American composers should be initiated with the life and works of William Wallace Gilchrist. In his day Gilchrist was a leading figure in music in Philadelphia and his influence extended beyond the borders of the city. Although he is mentioned everywhere in general histories of American music, very little has been known until now of his music and even less of his personal life.

Gilchrist spent most of his life in Philadelphia where he assumed a leading role in music affairs of the city. He organized the world famous Mendelssohn Club, a choral organization still in existence, and was instrumental in organizing performances of the music of his contemporaries as founder of the Manuscript Music Society (1891). He was sought after as a music teacher and his compositions were performed extensively during his lifetime.

Dr. Schleifer has captured in these pages the essence of the man and the late Victorian period in which he was active in Philadelphia.

Sam Dennison
Curator, Fleisher Collection
Free Library of Philadelphia

The life of William Gilchrist (1846-1916) has never been presented in detail, nor have his works been cataloged before now. Copies of music and documents are sparse and scattered, often difficult to find and sometimes not available at all, although there is evidence that they existed. Therefore, a general statement concerning the types of materials available and their locations has been included in this preface.

The libraries that contain the bulk of Gilchrist's music are the Library of Congress in Washington, D.C.; the New York Public Library at Lincoln Center; and the Free Library of Philadelphia. The Library of Congress card catalog has some Gilchrist entries, but most of his music is uncataloged and must be found by looking through boxes of sheet music. The music collection of the New York Public Library is organized by composer, but the card catalog is arranged by title and requests for music are made by title of the works. Gilchrist's music at the Free Library of Philadelphia includes orchestral works in the Fleisher Collection, chamber music in the Chamber Music Collection, songs in the song collection, and manuscripts that were given to the Library by Gilchrist's daughter, Anna. The Fleisher and Chamber Music Collections are cataloged by composer, and the songs are organized in alphabetical order by title. The Gilchrist manuscript collection is in alphabetical order according to genre, and I have listed the contents on index cards.

I searched the National Union Catalog, Pre-1956 Imprints, and the catalogs of the Public Library of the City of Boston and the Allen A. Brown Collection at the same repository; information from these is integrated into the works catalog. The John Hay Library at Brown University in Providence, Rhode Island, also contains a few works. The libraries of the University of Pennsylvania, Yale University and Harvard University list in their card catalogs only the entries in the National Union Catalog. The Historical Soci-

ety of Pennsylvania has some helpful materials including programs, a copy of the Gilchrist Memorial Circular and some
information concerning the Manuscript Music Society of Philadelphia.

Gilchrist worked at several churches in Philadelphia.
All church records at Saint Clement's Church during the time
that Gilchrist was organist and choirmaster there were destroyed by fire, and Christ Church in Germantown could offer no information. Gilchrist, a Swedenborgian by denomina-
tion, spent the longest part of his church career at the
Swedenborgian Church of the New Jerusalem at 22nd and
Chestnut Streets in Philadelphia, where there are copies of
a few individually published sacred works, but no manuscripts. There are two other Swedenborgian churches in
this area, the Lord's New Church and Bryn Athyn Cathedral.
The Cathedral has copies of several hymnals, the New
Church Messenger (a Church newsletter) and one Mendelssohn Club program, but the Lord's New Church has nothing,
and refers inquiries back to the other churches.

I also searched the catalogs and records of the United
States Copyright Office in Arlington, Virginia for titles and
publication information. I found additional titles listed on
published music in advertisements by the publisher. Programs found in scrapbooks, the program collections of the
Free Library of Philadelphia, and the Pennsylvania Historical
Society contain valuable information.

From 1878 to 1946, Anna R. Gilchrist (daughter of William Wallace) kept a scrapbook containing materials relating
to the Gilchrist family. She kept a ledger from 1913 to 1937
with information concerning sale prices, royalty rates, royalty
payments, and performance information for some of her father's music. She also attempted to list all of his compositions.
Although this list is very limited and sometimes incorrect it
does contain some information of value and provided a start-
ing point for the search for works. On this list Anna Gilchrist refers to manuscript books which have not yet been
located and in fact were probably misplaced or destroyed.
Anna also saved a journal kept during Gilchrist's European
trip which contains some original poetry, letters, a tribute
to Gilchrist from the Musical Fund Society, both a signed
manuscript and published copy of "A Maid's Choice," a copy
of Songs for the Children, and a published piano-vocal score

of the "Forty-Sixth Psalm" inscribed "Anna R. Gilchrist, from Pa." Various other members of the Gilchrist family lent me photographs and letters, and provided valuable information through correspondence and interviews. I located Gilchrist's surviving family members through the telephone book and by contacting known associates of the family now dispersed from Maine to California. Newspaper articles and obituaries were another source of information, and I conducted interviews with members of the Mendelssohn Club.

Much of Gilchrist's music was published by Theodore Presser Company, originally in Philadelphia, now in Bryn Mawr, Pennsylvania. Presser did not keep copies of music that it published (nor did any of Gilchrist's other publishers), but it does have a small folder of miscellaneous material relevant to Gilchrist from the Theodore Presser, John Church, and Oliver Ditson companies. These include agreements of sales, certificates of assignment, contracts, copyright certificates, financial statements, and letters. The other major publishers of his music were G. Schirmer in New York, Oliver Ditson in Boston and John Church in Cincinnati.

I would like to thank the many people who assisted in the creation of this work. Sam Dennison, the Curator of the Edwin A. Fleisher Collection at the Free Library of Philadelphia and my editor, encouraged this worthwhile project from its inception. Thanks to the staff of the music department of the Free Library, Mr. Frederick Kent, head of the department; and the staff of the music department of the Library of Congress, for assistance when it was needed and for allowing me to search for materials without interference. The staff at the Church of the New Jerusalem also gave as much information as they could.

Some of the grandchildren of William Wallace Gilchrist have been particularly generous and helpful. These include Mrs. Margaret Griffin (deceased), Mrs. Ellen Burbank, Miss Mary Daboll, and Mr. Edmund Gilchrist, Jr.

Sincere thanks go to my friend, Diana LeStourgeon, for the time and energy spent giving editorial assistance, proofreading, and moral support throughout the project.

My family deserves special thanks. My parents have always been supportive; my husband, Charles, has been proofreader, editor, general assistant and friend; and my children, Marc, David, and Daniel, have been proud, which provides support unequalled by any other.

William Wallace Gilchrist

Studio in Philadelphia

William Wallace Gilchrist was born in Jersey City, New Jersey, on January 8, 1846. His father, William, was a Canadian of Scottish descent born in Rivier-du-Loup, and his mother, Redelia Ann Cox, was an American born in New York State. In 1855, when William Wallace Gilchrist was nine years old, the family moved to Philadelphia, where Gilchrist's father had a business, which failed during the Civil War. The letterhead on a letter from William Gilchrist (signed Guvonor) to his son William Wallace Gilchrist, written December 30, 1862, reads "Wm. Gilchrist, Maker, Kerosene Lamps and Materials." Several years later in a letter to her son written on August 9, 1863, Redelia states: "...visions of former luxuries steal on me.... If your papa should meet with a good opportunity to transfer his business to New York, I should have no objection at all."

William Wallace Gilchrist's uncle, Charles Cox, wrote to him from New York on May 19, 1861, with news of the impending Civil War conflict and an invitation to visit:

> The excitement here, seems unabated. Everything speaks of war! and I think we'll have it, and what's more it is going to be a desperate one; but I hope, not a long one. If it does come to real fighting, there's an end of that abomination--slavery! Business is getting dull; some large houses are and have been shut up.... Things really look bad, but I hope you'll not let this fuss interfere with our July business, for I'd rather you could see the city now than if it were all quiet.... I calculate a grand time on the 4th, and I want you to be sure to be here on that grand day.

Gilchrist, although too young for the draft, enlisted in the Army with his older brother, James, a physician, in the spring of 1863. His mother wrote to him on July 12, 1863:

> Keep a cheerful, trustful spirit, and write a line to
> your mother now and then.... All our friends whom
> we have seen appear much pleased with your having
> gone ... and give you the credit of possessing pure
> patriotism, as you are not yet liable to the draft....
> Poor I, have often lamented that I could do nothing
> for my country; but now that I have two dear sons
> to stand up in her defence [sic], I am glad and
> proud, and have no need to lament the want of
> means. If such a thing should happen as that they
> should try to enduce you to serve longer than three
> months, I think you had better not; ... think of
> your mother as breathing a prayer from her heart
> for you.... Pray yourself too Willie ... trust in
> the Lord's good providence [sic] at all times; re-
> membering that while we are sincerely trying to do
> our duty he [God] allows nothing to happen to us
> which is not for our highest good.

In another letter, written to her son on July 23, 1863,
Redelia mentions Susie Beaman, Gilchrist's future wife, who
had come to visit:

> Susie Beaman is here, and will stay several days
> with us. She enquires kindly after you both [Wil-
> liam and James], and is one of the best and petti-
> est and most patriotic of girls.

Then on July 28, 1863: "Susie says if you will write and
suggest what she should say, she will write too." Redelia
continued to mention Susie in her letters that summer.

Gilchrist was ill while he was in the Army, and he com-
plained to his mother, who felt that Gilchrist's father should
try to help him get an early discharge. She wrote on August
1, 1863:

> I dispatch[ed] a note to your father ... asking him
> to write to Col. Day immediately and make the re-
> quest [for an early discharge]. I cannot think of
> having you get sick where you are, and I had no
> idea that you felt so poorly as you do.

William Gilchrist wrote for the discharge, and Redelia informed
her son of the request on August 4, 1863:

> You will have received, probably, a letter from papa
> ere this reaches you, informing you of his applica-
> tion to the Colonel & Captain for your discharge.
> We shall be impatient to hear the result; but it is
> very probable that we may all be disappointed. In
> such a case there is nothing for us to do but bear
> it as philosophically as possible. Very soon half the
> time will have expired.... Susie [Beaman] is still
> here, and as she enjoys being in the country, I
> have obtained her parents [sic] consent to her re-
> maining longer.... There is one thing I wish to
> caution you against my dear Willie, and that is, to
> be very careful how you find fault with those in au-
> thority over you. I regretted that you had written
> as you did in your last and one other letter ...
> about the probable motives of those who were keep-
> ing your regiment where you are. I know you did
> not mean any harm; but it does not sound well; and,
> among those who are already unfriendly to the Gov-
> ernment, it affords opportunities for unjust re-
> marks.... There may be causes for private com-
> plaint, and affairs may not always go on just as we
> think they ought to; still, it is the part of true
> patriotism to pass over all minor issues and keep
> our minds and hearts fixed on the great ends in
> view....

Because Gilchrist's family was not optimistic about an early
discharge Redelia wrote to him again on August 9, 1863,
referring to a letter from William:

> I suppose you have received your father's letter
> ere this, informing you that he has written ... to
> have you discharged. We hardly dare hope, though,
> to see you before your term is expired.

There is no evidence that Gilchrist was discharged early. After the Army he considered various careers including
business and photography, according to Rupert Hughes in
Contemporary American Composers (L.C. Page, 1900).
Charles Cox, Gilchrist's uncle, wanted William Wallace to join
him in a law firm in New York, but the young man's strong
interest and talent led him to a musical career. Gilchrist
studied voice, organ and composition with Hugh Clarke for
three years beginning about 1865. These three years with

Clarke were his only formal advanced music training, although he continued to study on his own. Hugh Clarke was
a Canadian who came to Philadelphia when he was twenty.
His music teacher was his father, James, a professor of music at the University of Toronto. James Clarke had a doc-
torate in music from Oxford and his father was a composer
in England. Hugh Clarke was appointed professor of music
at the University of Pennsylvania in 1875 and was awarded
a Doctor of Music degree there in 1887. He remained at the
University for fifty years. Years later, in a Philadelphia
Orchestra program for March 4, 5, 1910, Clark was quoted
as saying:

> I always felt confident that Gilchrist would make a
> mark as a composer, and the result has fully grati-
> fied my expectations, since every year adds to his
> fame. I am very glad to hear that his symphony
> is to be performed again by the Orchestra; it is a
> work that will surely grow in the estimation of all
> lovers of pure, sane music.

Gilchrist engaged in a variety of musical activities during
this early period. According to an obituary in the Boston
Transcript, December 31, 1916, from about 1867 to 1870 he
conducted a group of semiprofessional instrumental and vocal
performers called O.M.S.--Our Music Society. The obituary
also notes that he was a baritone soloist at Holy Trinity
Episcopal Church and at Saint Mark's Church in Philadelphia.

In 1868 he participated in a series of thirty-five light
operas planned over four years at the Amateur Drawing
Room, and in 1869 he sang with the Handel and Haydn Society and had leading parts in Messiah, Moses in Egypt, Judas
Maccabeus and a Stabat Mater. He was principally interested
in singing during this period, but he also played the piano,
organ and violoncello.

William Wallace Gilchrist and Susan [Susie] Beaman,
daughter of the Reverend E.A. Beaman, were married on
June 8, 1870, and the couple eventually had four children.
Anna, their only daughter, was born on May 29, 1871, while
the family lived at 322 North 32nd Street in Philadelphia;
Charles was born around 1874, Wallace in 1879 and Edmund
in 1885.

For a short period of time after they were married, Gilchrist and his wife lived in Cincinnati, Ohio, where Gilchrist taught in the Conservatory of Miss Bauer, according to F.O. Jones, editor of A Handbook of American Music and Musicians (1887). He was also organist and choirmaster of the First New Jerusalem Society Church in Cincinnati. After returning to Philadelphia (it is not clear exactly when), Gilchrist became organist and choirmaster in 1874 at Saint Clement's Episcopal Church where he founded the Mendelssohn Club from a group of male singers in the church choir. This group held an important place in Gilchrist's career. He also had two of his earliest songs published in 1874 by William H. Boner in Philadelphia. These songs, "When Thou Art Nigh" and "Sweetheart," were dedicated to his wife. Around 1877 Gilchrist became organist at Christ Church in Germantown until he moved to the Church of the New Jerusalem in Philadelphia. He was both organist and choirmaster at the Church of the New Jerusalem for many years and held the position of choirmaster until his death.

Gilchrist conducted many choral societies during his lifetime, including the Germantown Choral [society], the West Philadelphia Choral Society, the Harmonia, the Harrisburg Choral Society and in later years the Tuesday Club of Wilmington, Delaware. The Harmonia sent him the following letter on April 13, 1878:

> My dear Sir,
> Allow me on behalf of the Board of Directors of the Harmonia to ask your acceptance of the accompanying Works, as a slight acknowledgment of their obligation to you for your faithful and efficient conductorship of the Rehearsals of the Association during the past Season, and hoping our pleasant connection may be continued by a resumption of the same next Fall, believe me.

Gilchrist won prizes in composition beginning in 1878 when he won two competitions of the Abt Male Singing Society of Philadelphia for the best male choral piece. In 1880 he ranked third in the Cincinnati May Festival competition, and in 1881 he won three prizes from the Mendelssohn Club of New York for "Ode to the Sun," "In Autumn," and "Dreaming." Camille Saint-Saëns, Carl Reinecke, and Theodore Thomas were the judges for the Cincinnati Festival Associa-

tion competition at which Gilchrist was awarded a prize of
$1,000 in 1882. The prize composition was his setting of
the Forty-Sixth Psalm for solo, chorus, and orchestra, performed in Cincinnati on May 19, 1882.

Gilchrist had begun teaching at the Philadelphia Musical Academy around 1881 in addition to teaching privately.
In a letter to his wife sent from New York ca. 1881 he wrote:

> Have had several applications from people who want
> hours for lessons. And have no doubt I can have
> more teaching than I can do at larger prices, Zeck-
> wer [director of Philadelphia Musical Academy]
> wants more time too but I haven't promised any
> one--should like ... to save enough next year for
> us either to go to Europe, or begin to build a
> house.

In order to advertise, at this time Gilchrist had cards
which read:

> Mr. Wm. W. Gilchrist
> Is prepared to resume his lessons on the following
> terms, payable in advance:
> One quarter of twenty lessons (private) $50.00
> Classes of two persons $60.00
> Classes of three persons $75.00
> Address, 331 Hamilton St., or
> Care W.H. Boner & Co.,
> 1102 Chestnut Street.

He was honored on March 10, 1882, with a testimonial
reception and a gift of a watch by one of the choral groups
he conducted, the West Philadelphia Choral Society. Their
gift was accompanied by words of appreciation and a glowing
tribute to Gilchrist's musical abilities:

> ...Philadelphia, with all her Quaker conservatism,
> has given America ... a maestro.... We do indeed
> feel honored and proud that we are permitted to sit
> under your instruction from week to week.... We
> rejoice that your merits have been recognized by our
> sister societies, and we desire on this occasion to
> add our little tribute to those which have preceded
> us. Humble as this tribute is it comes from our
> hearts.

A Philadelphia Music Festival, held in May 1883, was arranged by Gilchrist with Charles M. Schmitz. Schmitz, a violoncellist, for several years conducted the Germania Orchestra (a local orchestra which existed from about 1860 to 1895), and was the music director at several Philadelphia churches during his lifetime.

Gilchrist wrote to his wife concerning the project on July 11, 1881:

> The Festival Board have offered S. and myself a certain salary of $1,250.00 with a percentage of profits, should there be any, which we have accepted. We have submitted our scheme. I will ... meet Music Com. [committee] and finally decide on programmes--make arrangements for purchase and publishing of music, select Rehearsal room, etc., etc. There is a mountain of work, all of which will have to be arranged for then, and as but few of the Directors have any experience, we will have to foresee everything.

In another letter, written at Upper Saranac Lake in New York State on August 22, 1881, he states that "If the Festival succeeds, I'll build one [a summer cabin]." That Gilchrist was involved in other activities in addition to the Festival at this time, he indicated in the same letter:

> I feel better everywhere but in my miserable old head than I have for years.... Don't get on your ear over that remark about my head. Don't insist my giving up Festival.... If I give up anything, it will be teaching. The thing that hurts me most ... is [not] writing, the thing I want to do most. There is more of that involved in Festival work.... Conducting is least troublesome and I have to earn a living somehow.

Gilchrist was an industrious person, always pushing to do more and more. He wrote again in the summer of 1882:

> Am crazy to get to work. My head is buzzing with themes and things--And if I settle down, I must write--I feel too selfish in staying away, and altogether I am a great trial to myself as well as to you.

> If I could only be sure of ten years good solid work
> to make up for what I have wasted--I think I could
> be satisfied--Just think, here I am 36, and what
> have I done compared to what I might have done--

The Philadelphia Music Festival did take place on May
9, 10, 11, and 12, 1883. The organization of 540, called the
Philadelphia Chorus, was made up of choral groups Gilchrist
conducted at the time, including the West Philadelphia Choral
Society, the Amphion Society of Germantown, and the Arcadian. In addition to the chorus there was a festival orchestra of 100 performers and soloists. The third evening
concert included Gilchrist's setting of the Forty-Sixth Psalm,
his prize composition from the 1882 Cincinnati festival.

THIRD EVENING CONCERT

OVERTURE--Magic Flute	Mozart
ARIA--"Che faro senza Euridice!"	
(Orfeo)	Gluck
ARIA--"Sound an Alarm!" (Judas	
Maccabeus)	Handel
ARIA AND CHORUS--"Inflammatus"	
(Stabat Mater)	Rossini

Intermission

SYMPHONY--No. 8 (The Unfinished) in	
B Minor, 1. Allegro moderato	
2. Andante con moto	Schubert
ARIA DI CHIESA--"Pieta, Signor"	Stradella
THE FORTY-SIXTH PSALM	Gilchrist

The enthusiasm of the chorus members and audience
encouraged the Board of Directors to plan a second festival.
Gilchrist and Schmitz directed the festival again on May 6,
7, 8, 9, 10, 1884, and Gilchrist was also a guarantor for the
1884 season. Many people wanted to join the chorus, but
according to the May 6-10, 1884, program, applications for
membership were turned down because the chorus was so
large. Statements from the programs in 1883 and 1884 ex-
plained the rationale of the Board of Directors:

> The value of such festivals in indicating ... the
> advance in skill on the part of Chorus and Orches-

> tra, in marking and improving taste of our audi-
> ence,-- ... listeners,--cannot be readily overesti-
> mated.
> In this short text lies the justification of what
> has been done in the past, of what is now doing,
> and of what will be undertaken in the future....

The Philadelphia Chorus continued to meet, but the
individual societies in it ceased to exist. The group participated in a concert for the benefit of the Beethoven Memorial
Association on February 28, 1888, and according to Robert
A. Gerson in Music in Philadelphia (Presser, 1940) it performed on April 24, 1890, an oratorio called "Jerusalem" by
Hugh Clarke, Gilchrist's teacher.

Gilchrist was an active member of the Music Teachers'
National Association (M.T.N.A.), a group concerned with
problems and standards of teaching. In 1884 Gilchrist attended an M.T.N.A. meeting in Cleveland and wrote to his
wife:

> We had a very successful meeting at Cleveland and
> the "American College of Musicians" is now estab-
> lished of which I was duly elected one [of] the
> first 18--"fellows"--It took an awful amount of talk-
> ing to get it through and a good deal of scheming
> to keep out the "Moody and Sanky [sic]" crowd [sup-
> porters of the evangelical singing-preaching duo], but
> we succeeded and seemed a very strong array of
> names. It will in time, be a good thing I hope, and
> bring the standard of teaching up, a good many pegs--

The American College of Musicians, organized under
the auspices of the M.T.N.A., was an agency for certifying
the professional proficiency of music teachers. The areas
included were piano, organ, voice, violin, theory, and eventually public school teaching; the system of examinations developed existed until 1895.

Gilchrist's choral work "De Profundis" was performed
at the M.T.N.A. meeting in 1884. He described the performance in an undated letter to his wife:

> As to the Pro, its reception was stunning--In the
> first place it was at the end of a 3-1/2 hour session

during which there had been essays and discus-
sions, so that the musical-programme didn't begin
until it seemed as though the people must be tired
out--but there was an evident desire to here [sic]
it and but few left. The other music was rather
coldly received by the audience which was made up
of material calculated to make a man wince a little.
Some of the very best men in the country--and
very critical all through--At the close of the first
movement, they came down like a thunder clap,
and fairly shouted, ditto for the second, and for
the third fairly rose to their feet--so of course I
had a chance to practice my bow again.... I could
have sold 50 copies right then--So you see I had
cause to be set up--I felt very much surprised I
must say--and can't yet quite make it out.... I
shall try to utilize the success, by stirring up Mr.
Schirmer some and other publishers--

According to Sumner Salter in "Early Encouragements to
American Composers" (Musical Quarterly, 1932), the Trio
in G minor was also performed during this meeting at a recital of American compositions on July 3, 1884.

Gilchrist continued to compose, conduct, and teach,
and his appreciative admirers honored him with another
Grand Testimonial Concert on January 15, 1886. Performances were by the Germantown Choral, one of Gilchrist's
groups, the Mendelssohn Club, and a variety of soloists.
Six of the thirteen compositions were by Gilchrist.

During the summer of 1886 Gilchrist travelled to Europe with
a group of people not including his wife or children. The
other members of the group have not been identified, but
Gilchrist and his wife must have known them well since he
often refers to them in a familiar manner in his letters. This
trip was apparently taken to broaden his outlook and experience although it imposed somewhat of a financial strain.
The group landed at Liverpool on May 29, 1886, and went
directly to Chester. The letters which Gilchrist wrote to
his family during this trip present a revealing picture of the
man. Gilchrist missed his family, and in a wedding anniversary letter to his wife on June 7, 1886, he wrote:

> It seems as if we had been away a year, and when
> I get a few minutes by myself which is pretty hard,
> I wonder how I am going to stick it out....

The travelers went through England to London, and
even though the pace of the tour was hectic, Gilchrist did
have some time to think about his life.

> Saturday we went to Westminster Abbey, as the
> most proper beginning--to morning service--found
> it a most delightful old place.... There is nothing
> like these old churches, and I am getting to be
> thoroughly in the spirit of them. We are too mat-
> ter-of-fact in our religious matters ... and--as I
> have before hinted are in danger of elevating our
> intellects at the expense of our emotions--Because
> emotions alone sometimes lead people astray, is no
> reason why they should be abolished--it is reason
> why they should be understood, and fostered in
> order to be understood--and I am getting to wel-
> come anything that stirs what I believe to be good
> emotions--I am awfully glad now that I came on this
> trip--I can see lots of things plainer than ever be-

> fore--and I think I shall do better work for it, and
> live a little better which, heaven knows! there was
> room for--There are lots of good people in the
> world beside us, and we make a big mistake in
> throwing away the whole of the old for in doing so
> we throw away good things--Their faults were more
> of expression than of emotion--.... England has
> been a revelation to me in a good many ways.
> Showing what man can do--for there really seems
> nothing left to be done--I look forward to Switzer-
> land as an illustration of what man can never ap-
> proach--to make even the slightest impression upon.

Gilchrist kept a handwritten journal of his European
trip which was eventually bound with some of his poetry.
On July 6, 1886, after ten days in London, he wrote in his
journal: "Last day in London!.... Allah be praised! I
have had enough of it, [London] and am in no hurry to re-
turn--." Gilchrist varied his activity by attending a cricket
match that day, a game which interested him since he played
cricket and tennis himself. Gerson in Music in Philadelphia
(Presser, 1940) noted that he had helped found the Belmont
Cricket Club in Philadelphia.

The party continued through Belgium to Germany,
spent a morning in Cologne, then took a Rhine boat to
Mainz, stayed overnight, and arrived on July 12 in Heidel-
berg, from which he wrote:

> Whether or not the trip here has paid, remains to
> be seen. I certainly have enjoyed it immensely and
> I think learned a good many things--formed a good
> many new opinions, and reformed a good many old
> ones--as to health. I still am far from sure that I
> would not have done better at home with Cricket,
> Tennis, etc. than with so much fatigue and excite-
> ment here.

The group arrived in Lucerne, Switzerland on July 15.
Gilchrist was annoyed because the people in the group spent
money on crowded first-class hotels instead of staying in
more interesting, less expensive ones. In a letter written
that day he said: "I don't want to get them to change their
style of living, which they enjoy, and I can't secede. So I
must grin and bear it." At the beginning of the trip he had

been doing well financially, but was now spending more than he had expected and was worried. In the same letter:

> I am sorry not to have sent you the money prom-
> ised, but things are mounting up so that I thought
> it wise to be provided for emergencies--the first
> part of the trip was not so expensive, but now
> they [traveling companions] appear to be getting
> reckless. I hope to be able to bring home enough
> to get on well with--So don't spend all you have--
> some things can wait a while. I know this kind of
> talk makes you miserable--and I had planned never
> to make you miserable any more but it needn't--I
> have plenty [of] business ahead--am gaining
> strength every day. Our expenses can be brought
> down in a smaller house, and I really think that
> even considering the waste (?) of this trip we shall
> be able to commence the season unusually well--

He was also concerned by the lack of time he had to write music and was making plans to change that.

> I have really made up my mind to one thing and
> that to cut down my teaching and if my throat
> withstand it come out again as a singer--Have sung
> some little lately and it seems to me as if my voice
> were getting better--I have sufficient reputation in
> the provinces--to get engagements, and I am anxious
> to try it.--The great incentive to this is that I will
> thus gain time to write, and that, I must do. Since
> being over here I have seen [in Europe] how much
> has been done, and how finished it all is, and thus
> been fired to do my part in the great work America
> has to do--

Gilchrist felt as though he had not accomplished much artistically even though he was involved in many activities. He reiterated this feeling in the same letter.

> Here am I 40 years old, and nothing really done--
> I must turn to and do it--If I hadn't an expensive
> family now, don't you see, I could go into two
> rooms, and be as poor as a mouse for the glorious
> cause of art. I guess it is better as it is though
> --Still I must work this winter. Last winter is a

horrible blank and must be forgotten--I suppose
you have Vol I of my diary by this time. You
needn't go into the sentiment of it if you don't
want to. It wasn't intended for any one but myself, and I don't believe you can appreciate it--
Above all don't bore the children with it--If I fail
in my mission I shall be consoled if there is some-
one to take it up--[son, Wallace]

He apologized for these complaints in a letter written
from Geneva on Thursday, July 22, 1886:

I feel so mean for having written you that blue letter from Lucerne that hear [sic] I am again writing, after only three days interval--I don't want
you to feel that I am not having the best kind of
a time, for I really am--The only disappointment is
that it is costing somewhat more than I had planned,
and the circumstances are such that I can't help it.
You will understand I guess that I don't object to
all this luxury, and rather accept it with good
grace--In fact, I take it as a compensation for the
money spent--and enjoy it to the very fullest ex-
tent. My throat has been decidedly better since
last report, and I think that the months rest at
Nazareth, [Susie and the children stayed in Nazareth, Pa. while Gilchrist was away] which I plan to
get will quite fix me up for the Winter--I am very
glad that I was in a manner forced to come--for it
has been a great benefit to me in a hundred ways
that don't appear on the surface.

The journey continued through Switzerland to Paris,
where the party arrived on July 23. As the journey drew
to a close Gilchrist wrote on July 25, 1886, from Paris:
"am spoiling for some work--actually need it--." The party
returned to London on July 27, and departed for home on
July 31. He wrote in his journal on July 29, 1886:

...on Saturday we enter upon that week of blank
monotony, which shall bring us home--This trip has
been a happy useful one, and I wouldn't willingly
part with one association it has given birth to--I
have learned much of the world, much of myself--
And I am thankful to say have more than my former
hope, for both--

Gilchrist travelled to Chicago in 1888, where a performance
of the Quintette in C minor, No. 1 was given according to
a letter written to his wife on July 1, 1888. That he had
some marital problems from time to time during his life is
hinted at in his early letters and is apparent again in a letter written on July 1, 1888,--"I really am homesick. But if
I get home safely am going to behave myself. You must
too."

   In 1891, Gilchrist founded the Manuscript Music Society, an organization which until 1936 encouraged the creation and production of new music in Philadelphia (discussed
more fully later). "A Maid's Choice, A Musical Pastoral" for
piano and speaking voice, illustrated by Howard Pyle, was
published in Harper's Monthly in 1891. The following year,
on March 20, 1892, the Symphony Society of Philadelphia was
organized and, according to a program of December 22, 1894,
chartered November 16, 1893. Gilchrist was the conductor
of this group. The program also provides the following information:

> The Symphony Society is composed entirely of ama-
> teurs who desire to demonstrate that the musical
> features of a large orchestra can be successfully
> accomplished in Philadelphia, and if the public will
> give it the needed support, such an orchestra will
> not only be a means of enjoyable entertainment to
> its Associate Members, but also afford opportunity
> to its Active Members for the study of the works
> of the best composers, and tend to foster in the
> general public an appreciation of the higher order
> of orchestral work, and be a means of educational
> development to its members such as could not oth-
> erwise be obtained.

By the December 22, 1894, concert the orchestra had

fifteen first and fifteen second violins, seven violas, six
cellos, four basses, two flutes, two clarinets, two oboes,
two bassoons, three horns, three trumpets, four trombones,
timpani, drums, and triangle. By 1899, when the Symphony
Society joined the Mendelssohn Club for the Gilchrist Testimonial, the orchestra had eighty men in it. Active members
paid no dues, but associate members did contribute to help
support the three concerts a year given at the Academy of
Music. The two top balconies of the hall were reserved for
music students, and rehearsals were open to students. The
concerts often featured soloists, and programs selected by
Gilchrist reflected both his knowledge of music and his
group's ability in addition to having audience appeal. The
program for April 20, 1895, which follows, featured Miss
Charlotte Maconda, Soprano soloist.

PROGRAM

1.	SYMPHONY, C major. "Jupiter"	Mozart
2.	JEWEL SONG, "Faust"	Gounod
3.	WEDDING MUSIC	Jensen
4.	SUITE NO. 2 "Peer Gynt," Op. 55	Grieg
5.	NYMPHES ET SYLVAINS	Bemberg
6.	OVERTURE. "Triumphal"	Rubinstein

The Society performed another important service by
bringing the Kneisel Quartet of Boston to Philadelphia.
This string ensemble played several concerts a year for over
twenty years in Philadelphia, beginning in 1896.

In 1899 Gilchrist wrote an article for the Musical Courier entitled "Philadelphia Singing Societies," in which he
stated the following: "It is safe to say that no amateur orchestra in this country has ever done such fine and well
sustained work" [Symphony Society]. An article in the
Philadelphia Public Ledger on February 27, 1910, stated:

> It is recognized that Dr. Gilchrist's work with the
> amateur association the Symphony Society of Phila-
> delphia ... laid the firm foundations of a desire
> for and an appreciation of orchestra music which
> resulted finally in the formation of the Philadelphia
> Orchestra....

To devote his entire time to the Mendelssohn Club,

Gilchrist resigned from the Symphony Society in 1889. An unidentified newspaper article from Anna Gilchrist's scrapbook contained the following explanation of his resignation:

> I left the Symphony ... because there was a small element among its directors which I thought, as it was lacking in musical symphony [sic], would not give me hearty support. The rivalry of the two clubs will be active but friendly, and the result of such competition can only be beneficial to the musical life of the city.
>
> While the Symphony was devoted exclusively to orchestral work, the field of the Mendelssohn will be both orchestral and choral music. Many persons are members of both organizations.
>
> As to my feelings toward the Symphony Society, there is nothing unkindly in them whatever. I have found out that the unsympathetic element in it was even smaller than thought, and it was almost entirely among the directors, for nine-tenths of the lay membership when they heard that I was going to leave signed a petition urging the directors to do all in their power to retain me.

Fritz Scheel, first conductor of the Philadelphia Orchestra, was at this time conducting a summer orchestra in a local park. An article in the Philadelphia Public Ledger on February 8, 1917, noted:

> In order to keep him in the city ... several employments were found for him. He was appointed conductor.... Mr. Gilchrist having resigned, of the Symphony Society....

No one will ever know if Gilchrist was forced to resign so that Scheel could be given the job as conductor of the Symphony Society in order to keep him in the city, although according to Frances A. Wister in Twenty-five Years of the Philadelphia Orchestra (Edward Stern, 1925), "Scheel had hesitated when asked to become leader of an amateur organization for fear of endangering his reputation." Scheel conducted the Symphony Society only for a season until the Philadelphia Orchestra was formed and the Symphony Society disbanded. The Society had a music library, which was sold to the Philadelphia Orchestra along with its timpani and music desks.

During its existence the Symphony Society met the
city's need for a symphony orchestra. When the Philadelphia Orchestra was formed, this need was fulfilled by an
orchestra that could go far beyond the limits of an amateur
group, no matter how ambitious and enthusiastic its members
and leaders were.

Gilchrist was involved in many other activities during
his years with the Symphony Society. On June 16, 1892,
he was awarded an honorary Doctor of Music degree by the
University of Pennsylvania. Although he often thought
about giving up teaching, he remained active in it despite
his complaints. A letter written in 1893 suggests that he
did indeed make time for teaching, as the stationery is
headed:

> Central Music School
> William Wallace Gilchrist, Director
> 107 South 15th Street
> Philadelphia

He also remained active in the Pennsylvania State Music Teachers' Association. At the annual meeting in 1893,
held in Scranton from December 27 to 29, two of his compositions were performed, "The Legend of the Bended Bow"
(cantata for mezzo-soprano and male chorus) and the Symphony in C major. In 1894 meetings were held in Harrisburg, Pennsylvania, where Gilchrist's "A Christmas Idyll"
was performed. Gilchrist was on the program committee for
the 1896 meeting, but none of his works was performed.

Gilchrist began conducting the Harrisburg Choral Society, Harrisburg, Pennsylvania, in 1895; the society performed Mendelssohn's "Elijah" at its first concert. In 1899
the Choral Society performed Gounod's "Redemption" accompanied by the Boston Festival Orchestra, which joined them
at subsequent music festivals. In 1908 the chorus and orchestra performed the "Erl King's Daughter" by Gade and
"Hora Novissima" by Horatio Parker. A review in the Harrisburg Telegraph on May 16, 1908, stated:

> Time was when such chorus singing in Harrisburg
> would have been a revelation--but in matters musi-
> cal we have taken immense strides forward....
> Under Dr. Gilchrist's skillful direction the society

takes front place among musical organizations in the State.

At the Testimonial Concert for Gilchrist in 1915 given by the Mendelssohn Club, the Harrisburg Choral Society presented Gilchrist with a loving cup accompanied by a complimentary letter, reprinted in a Mendelssohn Club Special Announcement, April 14, 1915:

> ...may the Harrisburg Choral Society which he helped to organize twenty years ago, and which he ably conducted for eighteen years share in this exceptional honor.... Our members grew to know Dr. Gilchrist so well that we considered him one of us. He was so earnest in his work; so faithful in the discharge of his duties; such a master of his profession; so patient with our shortcomings, and so affable and companionable.... He was no momentary enthusiast, but was a competent, consistent, conscientious conductor. Upon him our Society was built and upon him it has endured. This is literally the truth.
> Please present this loving cup to Dr. Gilchrist with the heartiest congratulations of our Society upon his worth as a man and musician, and our very best and sincerest wishes for his early restoration to health and renewed activities.

When Gilchrist died in 1916 the people of Harrisburg felt a great sense of loss. According to his obituary in the Harrisburg Telegraph, December 1916:

> Not only was the success of the Choral Society largely due to his ability, but he taught the people of the city a greater love for good music....

Gilchrist edited The Hymnal, officially adopted by the Presbyterian Church in the United States in 1895 and in 1902 by the Presbyterian and Congregational Churches, according to Robert Stevenson in the New Grove Dictionary of Music and Musicians (Macmillan Publishers Limited, 1980).

In 1896, Gilchrist was one of the Founders of the American Guild of Organists, an organization still in existence, whose main purposes were and still are the improvement of music in churches, high standards among organists, and exchange of information.

In 1897 music was introduced into the public school system of Philadelphia. According to the Report of the Superintendent of Public Schools for 1897, the "movable do" was used at the suggestion of Gilchrist and several other Philadelphia musicians. When it was founded in 1898, he became a member of the National Institute of Arts and Letters, an organization established for the furtherance of literature and fine arts in the United States, and in 1899 he contributed an article to the Musical Courier called "Philadelphia Singing Societies." Despite all these various activities, Gilchrist found time to compose a great deal of music, most of which was published and some of which was performed publicly.

Gilchrist was successful in his pursuit of high standards for himself and his groups. Although the organizations with which he was associated were always praised and admired, he was never quite satisfied. In a letter to his daughter, Anna, on June 21, 1904, he wrote, "Some day I hope to be connected with a successful venture--but it has got to hurry up--Have about concluded that I am the Hoodoo, but shall keep on fighting--." He seemed to have trouble composing that summer, too, and wrote to Anna on August 16: "My ideas seem very trite now a days, and I am doing nothing but writing pot-boilers--." In another letter to Anna, dated simply "summer, 1904," near the end of his vacation, "I'm O.K. too, and quite anxious to get home to work."

Gilchrist was bothered by his lack of financial success, but he did have a good sense of humor and was able to philosophize about his life, as he demonstrates to Anna in the "summer 1904" letter:

> Sorry you were disappointed in my great effort at letter writing--I didn't feel pessimistic especially--but a fellow cant [sic] get through a long life of ups and downs, without getting pretty serious--especially when the material results are so out of proportion to the effort expended, and the sacrifices made--I am however gradually getting more and more able to "rise above" these things, and look

complacently, if not cheerfully, and with a reestab-
lished sense of humor upon things generally. If
the boys [his three sons] do not make any money,
I am bound to say the causes of failure in that
line, lie in characteristics for which I admire them.
They certainly are unworldly and influenced by
considerations, too ideal for success, and if they
fail--it will be to their credit--Still I don't believe
they will fail. As I firmly believe in the ultimate
success though long delayed--of sincerity and ab-
stract truth--aside from all considerations of day-
to-day policy--This is the kind of success they
must have if they are to have any--and while it is
a long time coming--I am going on to the end ex-
pecting it--The lightest optimism is of this kind--
Even if in the details we seem pessimistic--Success
is built only on experience--which is another word
for daily failures.

Gilchrist's sons all became quite successful in their
respective fields. Charles was a mining engineer, a member
of the firm of Fairchild and Gilchrist, Civil and Mining En-
gineers, which made geological reports, developed mining
properties, and made surveys of various types. He was also
known for his daring and scientific mountain climbing ex-
peditions. Wallace was an artist, known especially for por-
trait painting. Edmund was a well-known, prolific architect,
whose papers are in the Library of the University of Pennsylvania. His father lived in a house especially designed
for him by Edmund.

Although at times Gilchrist wrote pessimistic letters,
he did have some of his own local fame and success. The
score for his Symphony in C major is in the Fleisher collection at the Free Library of Philadelphia, dated 1891. The
first performance of the work which can be documented took
place on May 17, 1892, at a joint concert of the Symphony
Society and the Manuscript Music Society. During its first
season the Philadelphia Orchestra performed Gilchrist's Symphony in C major on February 8 and 9, 1901. On this program was another American work, Edward MacDowell's Piano
Concerto, Number 2, with MacDowell as soloist. The Symphony was performed again by the orchestra on March 4
and 5, 1910. Carl Pohlig was the conductor of the concert,
but Gilchrist conducted his own composition. His work was

performed again on December 18, 1925, and at the Sesquicentennial Exposition in Philadelphia on the August 30, 1926,
program.   There have been recent performances of the work
by amateur orchestras, who have borrowed the score from
the Fleisher Collection in Philadelphia.

Philadelphia was saddened by the death of Fritz Scheel
in March of 1907.   In addition to conducting the Philadelphia
Orchestra Scheel had conducted two choruses, the Orpheus
Club and the Eurydice Chorus.   When Gilchrist was asked
to take over the choral groups until the end of the season,
he added the rehearsals and concerts of these groups to his
busy schedule.

Gilchrist's music was played often by such groups as
the Melody Club of Philadelphia, amateur musicians who had
Composers' Night programs in 1903 and 1904.   The programs
show that the 1903 concert included Gilchrist's Suite for
Violin and Piano, Number 1, and the 1904 concert, the Trio
for Violin, Cello and Piano.

Gilchrist's sacred cantata "Easter Idyl" was performed
for the first time in Philadelphia on April 18, 1907, by the
Mendelssohn Club at the Academy of Music.   The work had
been published in January and performed successfully in
Chicago before the Philadelphia première.   "Easter Idyl" was
enthusiastically received, and according to the Philadelphia
Inquirer, April 19, 1907,

> [it was a] work of moving eloquence, impressive
> dignity and true inspiration.   Its title ... does not
> communicate a just idea of the scope and character
> of the composition ... anything further removed
> from the idyllic than the subject ... or than the
> score, which is appropriately and poignantly re-
> sponsive to the theme could hardly be imagined....
> He is quite free from that tendency toward the
> sentimental which the modern composer is prone to
> exhibit and his music in its elevation, its ideality,
> its sobriety and its self-restraint is always worthy
> of its exalted theme.   It is melodious ... and its
> harmonies are always solemn rather than sensa-
> tional.   It is a work of real value and great inter-
> est, and the impression which it produced was so
> favorable that we may expect to hear it again.

A review in the Bulletin that day termed the "Idyl" a
"noble, impressive work" and the Public Ledger stated:
"The score, both vocal and instrumental, bore everywhere
the reflection of Doctor Gilchrist's scholarly attainments."
After the performance, Anna Gilchrist received a letter written on April 16, 1907, by her cousin, Polly Beaman.

> It is one of our dearest wishes for this slow old
> world to wake up and give Pops [Gilchrist] the
> support and appreciation due him during his life-
> time--it is sure to come and I trust he is to be
> here to enjoy it and to be encouraged by it. From
> what you write Philadelphians got well stirred up
> at that concert--If they appreciate this Idyl they
> will have added interest in what he has already
> done ... there is an originality and an appealing
> quality in it that precious little music has and how
> we wish we had been there, though I fancy it must
> have filled you all too full of feelings for comfort....
> I just ache to get acquainted with the Idyl, with
> the words now and sometime with the music....

Gilchrist wrote another Easter Oratorio, "The Lamb of
God," for the Good Friday service at the Church of the New
Jerusalem in 1908. The work was performed again at the
church in 1909. It was also performed at the Cathedral of
Saint John the Divine in New York City, where it was conducted by Walter Henry Hall in 1909. Hall conducted the
work again on March 21, 1917, when it was performed by
the Columbia University Chapel Choir. Hall, a professor of
choral music at Columbia, arranged for the publication of
the oratorio, which he believed to be a great American work,
according to his article, "W.W. Gilchrist: An Appreciation," (New Music Review, February 1917). The oratorio
was performed in Philadelphia again in 1925 at the First
Presbyterian Church (Washington Square) and at the Walnut
Street Presbyterian Church at a special service in 1933.
One of Gilchrist's anthems was also used in a service there
on April 2, 1933. In 1946, as part of the one hundredth
anniversary of Gilchrist's birthday, "The Lamb of God" was
performed at the Second Presbyterian Church in Philadelphia.

William Wallace Gilchrist was the first president and a
moving spirit behind the formation of the Musical Art Club

of Philadelphia, organized in January 1909 and incorporated
March 13. The club was a place for musicians to meet and
talk, to entertain visiting musicians, and to further the in-
terests of music in the city. It was a club specifically for
men, although ladies were allowed on some occasions. In
its original quarters at 17th and Chestnut streets there were
a reception room, billiard room, and dining room, in addition to business rooms. The club banned musical performance except under special circumstances, but every week
there was an ensemble night for members and all were encouraged to participate. Members included most of the
prominent musicians in the city as well as other men interested in the arts. A series of receptions honoring Philadelphia musicians and visiting musicians was given in 1909;
the first reception was in honor of Gilchrist.

At this point in his career Gilchrist was conducting
the Mendelssohn Club of Philadelphia, the Harrisburg Choral
Society, the Melody Club of Woodbury, New Jersey, and the
Choir of the Church of the New Jerusalem. He was president of the Manuscript Music Society and Musical Art Club,
in addition to teaching many students and composing.

In 1911 the Philadelphia Music Club presented a program of Gilchrist's music. This club was a very active wom-
en's group founded to further the careers of its members
and other Philadelphia musicians. The program included instrumental and vocal music by soloists, ensembles, and a
chorus, made up of members of the Woodbury Melody Club,
the Mendelssohn Club and the Philadelphia Music Club. The
Matinee Musical Club, a similar but older organization, held
a concert of music by Gilchrist on March 31, 1914. The
varied program included "The Fountain" and "Cherry Ripe,"
songs for women's voices; "Heart's Delight," for soprano;
Quintette, Number 2 in F, for strings and piano; "Blue
Eyed Lassie" and "Here Awa', There Awa'," for tenor;
"Serenade" and "Wynken, Blynken and Nod," for contralto;
and "The Sirens," a cantata for women's voices. This program by the Matinee Musical Club was probably in the nature of a testimonial to Gilchrist, similar to the others given
at this time in his life. Gilchrist had suspended many of
his activities because of what was called a temporary illness,
and many groups gave him tributes to show their love, support, and loyalty. The Musical Alumni Society of the University of Pennsylvania gave a testimonial concert of all Gil-

christ works on May 21, 1914, as did the Mendelssohn Club
with the Philadelphia Orchestra on April 14, 1915, and the
Manuscript Music Society gave an all-Gilchrist program November 29, 1916, and the Musical Alumni Society of the University of Pennsylvania. Although depressed, Gilchrist had
not stopped composing. He wrote two compositions for the
joint Philadelphia Orchestra/Mendelssohn Club concert, a
setting of the "Ninetieth Psalm" and a "Symphonic Poem."

Gilchrist was never able to resume all his many activities. He spent the last year and four months of his life in
the Easton (Pennsylvania) Sanatorium, suffering from "in-
volutional melancholia," according to his death certificate.
This condition is now known as depression and was probably
the illness which caused Gilchrist to discontinue most of his
work. The actual cause of his death was a heart attack
suffered on December 20, 1916. His wife, Susan, daughter,
Anna, and three sons survived. (Gilchrist's son, Edmund,
an architect, suffered a similar mental breakdown near the
end of his life.) Anna, who never married, became the administratrix of his estate, and it was she who discovered
the manuscripts which are now in the collection of the Free
Library of Philadelphia. Funeral services for Gilchrist were
held at his church, the Church of the New Jerusalem, and
he was buried in the churchyard of Saint Thomas' [Epis-
copal] Church on Bethlehem Pike in Fort Washington, Pennsylvania.

Gilchrist did not leave a will, but letters of administration named his daughter, Anna, as administratrix of the estate, which amounted to $623.91. Probably most of his property, such as the house in which the family lived at 8009 Crefeldt Street in the Chestnut Hill section of Philadelphia, was in his wife's name because when she died in 1931 her estate was valued at $19,035.89. Anna and her brother Edmund were executors of that estate. Anna lived with a sister-in-law at 1906 Sansom Street in Philadelphia until her death in 1953 at the age of eighty-two. Her estate was valued at $10,404.83.

At their concert on December 22, 1916, the Philadelphia Orchestra played Siegfried's Funeral March from Gotterdammerung in Gilchrist's memory. People immediately began planning memorials. Gilchrist and his various contributions to musical life and literature were praised in obituaries and editorials such as the following from the Philadelphia Inquirer on December 21, 1916:

> By common consent Dr. Gilchrist stood at the head of the profession which his talents and his character so brilliantly adorned. He stood there ... by the wide range and intrinsic value ... of his creative and interpretive abilities ... in the extent and originality of his intellectual endowment and of his artistic equipment, in the beauty of his conceptions, in the consummate skill of his workmanship, in the purity and elevation of the feeling by which his compositions were constantly and characteristically inspired, the man of whom our musical world has now been bereaved was quite without a peer.... There are some ... who have attained to a greater popularity ... for Gilchrist was too high minded a man and too true an artist ever to derogate [sic] from his ideals, and his native modesty, something

peculiarly refined and delicate and sensitive in his
nature, always restrained him from seeking to at-
tract a casual and adventitious attention.   In his
constitutional shrinking from whatever savored of
self-advertisement, Gilchrist often did himself in-
justice.... But ... the members of his profession
in common with all cultivated music lovers ... have
known that Dr. Gilchrist had taken rank among the
foremost of American composers.   Nor is it only as
a musician that Gilchrist's decease will be deplored.
By the many who enjoyed the privilege of his
friendship or acquaintance, he will be no less re-
gretted for the much that was lovable and admir-
able in his character.   If to be unselfishly, un-
flinchingly, unchangeably devoted to his ideals
constitutes the artist, if to be unfailingly consid-
erate of the rights and feelings of others marks
the gentleman, then no man ever better merited
those titles than he of whom these words are written.   Artist and gentleman William Wallace Gilchrist
was pre-eminently both.

The obituaries also noted his modesty and the help he
gave to his many students.   Walter Henry Hall, who wrote
an "Appreciation" of Gilchrist in the New Music Review
(February 1917) shortly after he died, felt that perhaps if
he had not been so "shy and retiring" Gilchrist might have
made himself known to more people, but that was not his
way.   Hall continues:

The possession of the creative gift would not alone
sufficiently explain the affection in which Dr. Gilchrist was held by Philadelphians.   It was his rare
personality which bound him to all with whom he
came in contact.

According to an article in Musical Philadelphia in February
1917,

His influence for the betterment of those with whom
he came in contact, though quiet, was most po-
tent....   He cared not to be great ... but subor-
dinated self that he might serve well mankind and
the cause of music.

The Musical Fund Society, established in 1820, to provide "relief and support [for] decayed musicians and their
families," and to elevate musical taste, printed an "In Memoriam" booklet, "Tribute to William Wallace Gilchrist from the
Musical Fund Society."

> The Board of Directors of the Musical Fund Society
> have learned with sincere regret of the death of
> Doctor William Wallace Gilchrist and recognizing him
> as one of the foremost musicians of the City of
> Philadelphia, and America, desire to express their
> profound appreciation of his musical abilities, as
> well as the great service he rendered to the cause
> of music, as a composer, as well as a teacher and
> conductor....

Soon after his death a fund was established for a memorial to Gilchrist. A circular, William Wallace Gilchrist Memorial, dated February 17, 1917, and describing the memorial,
was sent to many people who had been associated with Gilchrist. It called Gilchrist a leading figure and power in music in Philadelphia:

> It is felt to be an urgent public duty that the
> memory of such a man be not allowed to lapse into
> obscurity.... While it is difficult to judge the
> precise value of contemporary art, many musicians
> who know the larger works of Dr. Gilchrist are
> convinced of their enduring beauty and greatness
> of conception.

The memorial suggested was a medallion in the Academy of
Music, music scholarships at the University of Pennsylvania
and possibly the publication of some manuscripts.

Although most of the musicians in the city gave public and financial support to the project, unfortunately the
funds collected did not reach expectations. Finally, in 1921
a bas-relief of Gilchrist by Louis Milione, a well-known
Philadelphia sculptor, was erected in the Academy of Music,
and the Philadelphia Orchestra programs for April 29 and
30, 1921, included his "Symphonic Poem" as a memorial
tribute. Following his death additional programs of Gilchrist's music were performed, such as the spring concert,
June 4, 1917, by the Musical Alumni of the University of

Pennsylvania, which included the Fantasie for Violin and
Piano. The Matinee Musical Club on February 3, 1929 presented a program by Pennsylvania composers which included
two songs by Gilchrist, "Heart's Delight" and "Dainty Davie."

In the early 1930's Anna Gilchrist discovered that her
father had written another symphony, which he had apparently sent to an orchestra in the Midwest soon after the
work was finished. The symphony was lost and Gilchrist
never reconstructed it, but he kept all of the sketches and
many of his manuscript notes written during the creation of
the work. When Anna found this material she brought it to
Edwin A. Fleisher, who sent it in 1933 to William Happich
for examination. Happich was a violinist on the staff at
Temple University and conductor of the Symphony Club.
The Symphony Club, founded in 1909 by Edwin A. Fleisher,
a wealthy Philadelphia business man, is still in existence.
The club is an amateur orchestra that devotes half of each
rehearsal to sight-reading music and therefore requires a
large library of music scores. Through Fleisher's generosity
the internationally known "Fleisher Collection" housed in the
Free Library of Philadelphia was established so that enough
music would be available for the use of the orchestra. The
collection includes standard orchestral works and manuscripts
of many unpublished compositions now used by orchestras
around the world.

Happich was able to reconstruct the Symphony in D
major (second) from material Anna Gilchrist gave him. He
wrote to Anna on April 4, 1933:

> My dear Miss Gilchrist--
> The manuscript parts to your father's II Symphony
> were finished last week. We have been working
> some on it, and we are giving it a thorough re-
> hearsal this week, with a view of playing it for Mr.
> Fleisher as a surprise on Thursday of next week,
> April 13th, 8 P.M.

Anna noted on the back of the letter that she had attended
the private concert with her brother and a few other guests.
In 1936, after Fleisher told the Music Committee of the Art
Alliance about the work they arranged for it to be performed at a joint concert for the Art Alliance and the University of Pennsylvania; it was performed by the Fleisher

Symphony Concert Orchestra on Friday, April 9, 1937, at
Irvine Auditorium.

In 1936 the Civic Symphony Orchestra was established
by the Works Progress Administration (W.P.A.) Federal Music Project in Philadelphia. It was directed by J.W.F. Leman, who was also the director of the Composers' Forum
Laboratory, a division of the project which was devoted to
playing the works of local composers, similar to the Manuscript Music Society, founded by Gilchrist. Leman wrote to
Gilchrist's son Edmund on August 6, 1936:

> ...I am thinking of presenting several memorial
> programs, that is: compositions of outstanding
> composers of the near past who have been out-
> standing contributors to Philadelphia's musical de-
> velopment. Particularly I am thinking of your
> father, with whom I played so often.
>   Could you supply me with a list of your father's
> outstanding compositions, and could you supply the
> orchestral compositions, and could you supply the
> orchestral parts to some of his orchestral works
> especially his Symphony which I think I played with
> the Philadelphia Orchestra years ago?

The Civic Symphony Orchestra program for February
7, 1937, included Gilchrist's "Symphonic Poem." Leman arranged a W.P.A. Composers' Forum Laboratory recital of
works by Philadelphia composers for May 21, 1937; the recital included Gilchrist's Fantasie for violin and piano and
two solo songs, "Here Awa', There Awa'" and "How Many
Thoughts." The Symphony in C major, Number 1, was performed by the Civic Symphony Orchestra on February 20,
1938, at Mitten Hall, Temple University, with Leman conducting.

On January 11, 1940, the Mendelssohn Club and the
Philadelphia Orchestra gave a testimonial concert of Gilchrist's works, which included the "Ninetieth Psalm." The
Philadelphia Chapter of the National Association of American
Composers and Conductors presented a program on January
11, 1943, which included the Quintette in F major, Number
2.

The centennial of Gilchrist's birth did not pass un-

noticed.   Gertrude Trauble, a Philadelphia singer, wrote to
Anna Gilchrist on December 16, 1945:

> I am singing a little song of your father's "Spring
> Grasses" as my small contribution to celebrate his
> one hundredth birthday anniversary....   The oc-
> casion is my annual recital for children ... Frances
> McCollin [Gilchrist's student] thought you might
> like to come and I hope you will.

One of the Philadelphia newspapers, the Evening Bulletin, on January 8, 1946, one hundred years after Gilchrist's birth, carried an article about the composer's musical career.   The music for the services on January 13 at the
Church of the New Jerusalem was all by Gilchrist, including
the hymns and liturgical responses.   The music was under
the direction of Elizabeth I. McCloskey, a pupil and assistant of Dr. Gilchrist, who was a soprano soloist during a
part of his term as music director of the Church and suc-
ceeded him in that role.   Selections included "Ponder My
Words" and "O Lord Thou Hast Searched Me Out," for choir
and the "Andante in C" for organ.   There was a performance
of the "Lamb of God" at the Second Presbyterian Church,
21st and Walnut streets in Philadelphia, on March 17, 1946.
The anthem for the Easter Service at the Church of the
New Jerusalem was Gilchrist's "Behold now, Fear ye not,"
and the Mendelssohn Club included "Cherry Ripe" on its
May 1946 program.

Gilchrist's music has been neglected since his death,
but as a result of the Bicentennial there appears to be a
revived interest in American music which extends to his compositions.   The Nonet score was borrowed from the Free Library of Philadelphia for performance at the Newport Music
Festival in August 1975.   The Symphony in C major, Number
1, was borrowed and performed by the Chestnut Hill Symphony in Philadelphia in 1975 and by the Old York Road
Symphony in Abington, Pennsylvania, in 1982.   The Quintette in F major, Number 2, was performed in January 1976,
at Haverford College, Haverford, Pennsylvania, by the de
Pasquale String Quartet with Sylvia Glickman, pianist.

It is to be hoped that interest in the music of Gilchrist
and other American composers will continue to increase and
performances of their works will occur more frequently than
they have in the recent past.

The Mendelssohn Club of Philadelphia came into existence in 1874 as a group of eight male singers selected from Gilchrist's choir at St. Clement's Church in Philadelphia. In 1875 eight men were added and the club was formally organized. Gilchrist conducted the first subscription concert on December 11, 1879, at Saint George's Hall with a chorus which had grown to include ten sopranos, six altos, six tenors and seven basses. The program, which is contained in the Gilchrist scrapbook, follows:

PART FIRST

1.	CHORUS--"Hunting Song"	Henry Smart
2.	SOLO, for Violoncello--"Sous le balcon"	Lee
3.	SEMI-CHORUS FOR FEMALE VOICES-- The Sea-Fairies	Gilchrist
4.	CHORUS--"Break, break, break!"	Macfarren
5.	PIANO SOLO-- (a) "Prelude" (b) "La Polka Glissant"	Chopin Raff
6.	SOLO AND CHORUS--"An Elegy"	Raff

INTERMISSION

1.	CHORUS-- (a) "Hence loathed melancholy" (Prize Glee) (b) "May Song"	Lahee Franz
2.	SOLO FOR VIOLONCELLO (a) "Romance" "Ich denke dein" (b) "Musette"	Schreiner Offenbach
3.	SEMI-CHORUS FOR MALE VOICES--	

              (a) "Tell me on what holy
                    ground?"   Fuss
              (b) "Song of Harold Harfager"   Werner
        4. FINALE TO FIRST ACT OF
              "LORELEY"   Mendelssohn

Words for the vocal selections on the first part of the program and the Mendelssohn work were included on the program.

"The Uplifted Gates" by Gilchrist was included in the
March 28 and May 1, 1883, concerts. (The work was also
performed at the Gilchrist Testimonial, January 15, 1886,
given by various groups including the Mendelssohn Club.)
The May 1883 program carried the following notice:

> The subscription book for the concerts of the
> Mendelssohn Club, ... has been opened at Boner's
> Music Store, 1102 Chestnut Street. Application
> can also be made to any of the Active Members.
> Subscription Price (three seats for each of three
> concerts), $5.00.

The March 28, 1883, concert included other choral
works, two violin solos and two works for two pianos, one
for eight hands by Moscheles called "Les Contrastes" and a
Rondo Op. 73 for four hands by Chopin. For variety, Gilchrist usually added to the program an instrumental work
performed by a guest soloist.

The program for the first subscription concert of the
fifteenth season, December 16, 1890, included a list of 270
associated members; this kind of support by the people of
Philadelphia contributed to the success and longevity of the
club. Thomas A'Becket, Jr., a long-time supporter of the
Mendelssohn Club, was the pianist for this concert, which
had three solo violin pieces on the program. Gilchrist began with the "Utrecht Jubilate" by Handel and ended with
his own arrangement of "Ring Out, Wild Bells" by Gounod
for chorus and four hand piano accompaniment.

In 1899 an orchestra was added to the Mendelssohn
Club and the Choral group was enlarged. The orchestra
appeared at many of the concerts, but in 1903 it was disbanded and the Mendelssohn Club again confined itself to
choral activities.

Another Testimonial Concert was given for Gilchrist
on May 11, 1899, by the Mendelssohn Club and the Symphony Society of Philadelphia. The announcement for the
concert stated:

> The object in giving this Concert is to show their
> appreciation of the excellent work Dr. Gilchrist
> has accomplished for each organization, he having
> been conductor of each society since its inception,
> and by persistent, faithful work has done inesti-
> mable good to both organizations.... Dr. Gilchrist
> has taken a leading part in the musical history of
> Philadelphia for the past quarter of a century, and
> his high professional attainments and personal es-
> teem make him worthy of the fullest expressions of
> public appreciation in the coming Testimonial Con-
> cert.

Programme

1.	42nd PSALM	Mendelssohn
2.	SYMPHONY. B minor (unfinished)	Schubert
3.	TENOR SOLO. "Spring Song" (Die Walkure)	Wagner
4.	a. TRAUMEREI and ROMANCE (String Orchestra)	Schumann
	b. SUITE No. 1. "Carmen"	Bizet
5.	TENOR SOLO	
	a. "Safe in Silence"	Franz
	b. "O Lay Thy Cheek"	Jensen
	c. "The Message"	Brahms
6.	GALLIA	Gounod

An article by John Lawes, "Gilchrist Honored," in The Item,
May 12, 1899, criticized the programming because it did not
include any works by Gilchrist.

> ...the testimonial concert was a brilliant success.
> Those who were there were evidently enthusiastic
> admirers of Mr. Gilchrist ... they gave the com-
> poser-conductor one of the greatest receptions ever
> accorded a musician.... No one has done as much
> --in a musical way--for Philadelphia music.... He
> has worked hard, faithfully and well in his efforts

to establish music on a thoroughly classical basis, finding time in between these efforts to give to the world some most excellent compositions. The pro- gramme submitted was an excellent one saving for one in-excusable feature. There was not a single one of Mr. Gilchrist's own compositions.... With the many beautiful selections that Mr. Gilchrist has written for orchestra, with the quality of excellent numbers that he has given out in the way of part songs it does not seem possible that such an error could be made.

The concert was opened by Mendelssohn's set- ting of the 42nd Psalm. Why not Gilchrist's prize setting of the 46th or any other of his sacred sub- jects?

An article in the Evening Telegraph praised Gilchrist:

[The Testimonial] was a proper recognition of an artist who stands deservedly high in ranks of this city's musicians. Dr. Gilchrist has done a big work in Philadelphia, and has done it with such modesty and entire absence of selfishness and of- fensive advertising, as to win the respect ... of the musical public.

The Press alluded to his lack of financial gain despite his many activities and hard work.

Although his silver jubilee represents a period of great activity, much of the work done has been without return save in the satisfaction of having been part of the newer and better musical life of Philadelphia.

A publicity flier of press comments in the Gilchrist scrap- book contains excerpts of articles about the Mendelssohn Club's activities from March 7, 1902, to June 14, 1904. An article quoted from the Public Ledger, December 19, 1902 states:

The chorus has done most excellent work ... and is steadily increasing in public estimation. There is no better organization for the interpretation of part songs to be heard here.

Another quotation from the Bulletin, December 19, 1902:

> The Mendelssohn Club opened its 28th season ...
> with a concert which was so notably and so remark-
> ably perfect in all respects.... Mr. W.W. Gilchrist
> has brought his large body of singers to such a
> state of efficiency in the rendition of the part
> songs ... it is doubtful if there is ... a mixed
> chorus to excel them in this particular line.

From the North American, March 6, 1903:

> The Mendelssohn Club has for many years ...
> achieved notable results, born of long practice,
> unity of ideals, and harmonious co-operation.   In
> precision of attack, oneness of voice, perfection of
> staccato, and smooth, finished performance, the
> Club stands unequalled among American organiza-
> tions.

The group was also received enthusiastically outside of Philadelphia.   After a performance in Atlantic City, New Jersey, the Atlantic City Review, June 15, 1904 wrote:

> No higher order of classical music in a Chorus of
> mixed voices has ever been heard in Atlantic
> City....   The numerous voices blended in beautiful
> harmony, showing the assiduous application of the
> director, Dr. W.W. Gilchrist, in carefully preserv-
> ing the exact balance of the chorus.

Gilchrist was quite concerned with the success of the
Mendelssohn Club.   In 1903, after a meeting concerning the
performance of Beethoven's Ninth Symphony with the Philadelphia Orchestra he wrote a letter to a club member on
March 15.   "... the success of the M.C. is my one ambi-
tion....   A good deal [additional performances with the orchestra in the future] depends on our success....   I am
particularly anxious that he [Fritz Scheel, conductor of the
Philadelphia Orchestra] should have a good opinion of the
club."   This letter was sent with the following note to Gilchrist's daughter after her father died:

> Dear Miss Gilchrist:
> Enclosed is the letter from your father that I spoke

to you about yesterday. I can visualize your father perfectly as he was during my ten years of membership in the Club--his beautiful sensitive face and his boundless enthusiasm for the success of the Club. How we all loved and admired him.
Yours most sincerely,
Annie L. Maclaughlin

The club sang with the Philadelphia Orchestra on January 2, 1904, and performed Beethoven's Ninth Symphony with the orchestra at two more series of concerts during Gilchrist's lifetime, February 7, 8, 1907, and March 13, 14, 1914. It also performed with the Philadelphia Orchestra during the 1902-1903 Popular Concerts Series in a program which included Brahms' "Ave Maria" for women's voices, Goetz' "Noenia," and Gounod-Gilchrist's "Nazareth." In addition the Mendelssohn Club joined the Philadelphia Orchestra again for one of Four Gala Concerts for the Guarantee Fund given December 29 and 30, 1911. It sang Brahms' "Veneta" and "The Autumn"; a Serbian folk song, "Evening on the Sava"; Schumann's "Gypsy Life"; Wagner's "Wach Auf" and "Ehrt eure deutschen Meister," from Act 3 of the Meistersinger; Tchaikowsky's "Legende"; "Three Old Bohemian Christmas Carols"; and Gilchrist's arrangement of Gounod's "Nazareth."

On January 23, 1908, the club sang the Philadelphia première of Brahms' German Requiem. An article in the Public Ledger on January 24, 1908, indicated that the work had been performed in New York about thirty years before, then in Cincinnati in the 1880's. Until the 1908 performance it had been neglected by Philadelphia musicians.

Gilchrist's cantata, "Easter Idyl," was performed for the first time in Philadelphia on April 18, 1907, by the Mendelssohn Club, assisted by an auxiliary chorus and orchestra. The reviews in the Philadelphia Inquirer and the Bulletin compared the "Idyl" to Bach's sacred music. By this time active members of the club included thirty-three sopranos, thirty-four altos, sixteen tenors and twenty-seven basses. The following year the first Philadelphia performance of Sir Edward Elgar's "King Olaf," assisted by an orchestra made up of members of the Philadelphia Orchestra, was given by the club on April 23, 1908. The soloists were Mrs. E.M. Zimmerman, soprano; Mr. Daniel Beddoe, tenor; Mr. Henri G. Scott, bass.

The North American (Philadelphia) on January 17,
1909, published an article with photographs of Mendelssohn
Club members. It praised the club for its dedication and
contributions to music in Philadelphia and noted that sometimes members' contributions to the Mendelssohn Club were
financial as well as musical. Gilchrist's choice of music was
noted as being ambitious, and he was commended for maintaining high standards of performance.

> Its members declare freely that if this were a coun-
> try wherein there was governmental recognition of
> artistic superiority their leader would have long
> since been decorated and knighted, as for instance
> Sullivan and Elgar in England.

A Mendelssohn Festival was held at the Academy of Music in
Philadelphia on April 20, 1909, to commemorate that composer's one hundredth birthday. The festival chorus of 750
voices, a full orchestra and soloists, directed by Gilchrist
and Henry Gordon Thunder, performed Mendelssohn's "The
First Walpurgis Night" and "The Hymn of Praise." The
large chorus was made up of the Choral Society of Philadelphia, Henry Gordon Thunder, director; the Mendelssohn
Club; the Schubert Choir of York, Pennsylvania, Henry
Gordon Thunder, conductor; and the Church Choral Society
of Reading, Pennsylvania, Edward Kneer, conductor.

Subscription concerts continued to include instrumental soloists and frequently in order to support the abundance
of talent in the city Gilchrist chose Philadelphia musicians as
soloists. He also programmed the music of local composers
which he considered suitable for the Mendelssohn Club.

In 1910 Gilchrist celebrated his thirty-fifth year with
the Mendelssohn Club; a supplementary prospectus for the
season announced:

> In order to fitly recognize the completion of the
> 35th year of Dr. Gilchrist's continuous leadership
> of the Mendelssohn Club, the Treble Clef [women],
> Mr. Samuel L. Herrmann, conductor, and the Or-
> pheus Club [men], Dr. Horatio W. Parker, con-
> ductor, were invited to assist at the last concert
> of the series to be given on Thursday evening
> April 28, 1910. Each of these organizations cordial-

ly accepted the invitation and will be represented on the program by groups of part songs led by their own Conductors, as well as uniting with the Mendelssohn Club in a mass chorus with Dr. Gilchrist conducting.

This occasion will afford a rare opportunity of hearing at one time representatives of the highest development of choral singing, each in its chosen field.

The Mendelssohn Club earnestly solicits the support of its former subscribers as well as of all who are in sympathy with the high ideals it has so consistently striven to realize under the leadership of its honored Conductor.

The long program on April 28, 1910, ended with the three groups combined under the direction of Gilchrist in a performance of his arrangement of Gounod's "Nazareth." Public reaction to this concert and to the Mendelssohn Club in general was highly complimentary. A short newspaper clipping in the Gilchrist Scrapbook noted that:

There are few cities that can boast of such an able and efficient group of singers.... The Mendelssohn Club has consistently stood for what is highest and best in part-song singing and the rendition of concerted works.... This established record has only been brought about by the conscientious and painstaking efforts of Dr. Gilchrist who has maintained the club's standard of excellence through the past thirty-five years.... The Mendelssohn Club ... is a living monument to the faithful and painstaking labors of Doctor Gilchrist.

During the next three seasons Gilchrist conducted the club by maintaining his high standards of programming and performance, but a Mendelssohn Club revised prospectus for the 1913-1914 season announced that:

Owing to the continued illness of our conductor, DR. W.W. GILCHRIST, the Board of Directors has granted him an indefinite leave of absence.

Because Gilchrist became very depressed during 1913 he suspended most of his activities, but he continued to com-

pose. Although Herbert J. Tily was appointed acting conductor for the 1913–1914 season, the program for December
18, 1913, carried an announcement which indicated that Gilchrist expected to conduct the third concert, a joint effort
of the Mendelssohn Club and members of the Manuscript
Music Society. The concert on May 7, 1914, was made up
of compositions by the Manuscript Music Society of Philadelphia, beginning with Gilchrist's "Ave Maria" for chorus
and concluding with three more of his works, "The Blue-
Eyed Lassie" and "Here Awa', There Awa'" for tenor and
"The Rose" for chorus. The Gilchrist works were conducted
by Herbert J. Tily since the composer was not well enough
to resume his position, and the other choral works on the
program were conducted by the men who composed them.

    Since Gilchrist was appreciated by many people in
Philadelphia who wanted to give him moral support during
this difficult period of his depression, several groups gave
testimonial concerts in his honor. The Musical Alumni Society of the University of Pennsylvania gave a Testimonial
Concert on May 12, 1914. The announcement read:

> It is not well known that Dr. Gilchrist received
> his [honorary] degree from the University of Penn-
> sylvania. It is now a fitting time for the Univer-
> sity to join in public recognition of one of its most
> illustrious sons who has done so much for musical
> culture in Philadelphia and who reflects such
> credit on the University. Philadelphia does not al-
> ways fully recognize or appreciate its own institu-
> tions or its native workers who are more often
> thought of outside of the city than in it. The
> program has been arranged so as to show Dr. Gil-
> christ's splendid versatility....

The Mendelssohn Club sang the choral works accompanied
by H. Alexander Matthews; Gilchrist was listed as the conductor, Tily as the acting conductor. Other artists who
performed were Frederic Hahn, first violinist; Lucius Cole,
second violinist; J.W.F. Leman, viola; Carl Kneisel, violoncello; Agnes Clune Quinlan, pianist; Abbie R. Keely, soprano; John B. Becker, tenor; J. Harry Wadlow, baritone.
The program, presented at Houston Hall, 34th and Spruce
Streets, on Thursday, May 21, 1914, was made up entirely
of Gilchrist's works.

PART FIRST

1. CHORUSES — a. The Club Motto / b. Ave Maria
2. TENOR SOLO — a. How Many Thoughts / b. Here Awa', There Awa'
3. CHORUS — In the Blush of Evening (Women's Voices)
4. SOPRANO SOLOS — a. Thou'rt Like Unto a Flower / b. Heart's Delight
5. BARITONE SOLO (with Cello Obligato) Reverie
6. QUINTETTE

PART SECOND

1. CHORUS — The Uplifted Gates
2. SOLO — O Lord, Thou Hast Searched Me Out
3. CHORUS (with Alto Solo) — The Rose
4. SOLO — My Sins, My Sins, My Saviour
5. CHORUS — Nazareth

The Mendelssohn Club Prospectus for the 1914–1915 "Fortieth Anniversary and Testimonial Season" listed Gilchrist as conductor:

> During all this time the Club has had but one Conductor, Dr. W.W. GILCHRIST, under whose inspiring leadership a new and higher standard of choral excellence has been established and maintained. On account of ill health Dr. Gilchrist was unable during the past season to conduct the Club at any of its public performances. While now much improved, his medical advisers deem it unwise for him to attempt, at this time, to take up the work of conductor.

Gilchrist recommended the appointment of Charles E. Knauss

as acting conductor. The anniversary concert on Wednesday
April 14, 1915, was announced as a testimonial to Gilchrist,
and the artists who participated volunteered their services
so that the profits of the season could be given to Gilchrist.
They included the Philadelphia Orchestra and conductor,
Leopold Stokowski; Marie Kunkel Zimmerman, soprano; Marie
Stone Langston, contralto; Nicholas Douty, tenor; Edwin
Evans, baritone. The program was composed entirely of
works by Gilchrist including two written especially for this
occasion, "Symphonic Poem" for orchestra and the "Ninetieth
Psalm" for solo quartette, chorus and orchestra. Also on
the program were "The Club's Motto" for chorus and or-
chestra, two part songs, and two tenor solos.

Several Philadelphia newspapers published articles and
editorials both before and after the concert on April 14,
1915. An editorial in the Public Ledger on April 10, 1915,
exclaimed that:

> ...[Gilchrist] has done more than any other man
> for the advancement of the musical interests of
> Philadelphia. No Philadelphia musician begrudges
> him this spontaneous testimonial or fails to feel the
> pathos of the fact that protracted illness prevents
> the attendance and the personal participation of
> him whom Philadelphia honors itself in honoring.
> Doctor Gilchrist has done so much and done it so
> nobly, for Philadelphia that the whole musical frat-
> ernity rises to acclaim the man and his life work
> ... [he is] one of the few American composers
> whose lasting fame is assured by their handwork.

During the 1915-1916 season Gilchrist was again listed
on the Mendelssohn Club programs as conductor while Knauss
remained acting conductor. The prospectus for 1916-1917
also listed Gilchrist as conductor, but announced the appointment of N. Lindsay Norden as acting conductor. Norden was the club conductor after Gilchrist's death until
1927.

The Mendelssohn Club did not forget Gilchrist after
he died. They sang his "Day is Gently Sinking" and "Here
Awa', There Awa'" as a memorial to him at the January 18,
1917, concert, and at the fiftieth anniversary concert on
February 11, 1925, they sang "The Uplifted Gates." An arti-

cle in The Helper (1936), a weekly publication by the New
Church Book Center, noted that on February 9, 1936, the
club was heard on national radio for the first time, singing
as the first composition its motto, "Ode to Song," words
and music by Gilchrist. Gilchrist's daughter, Anna, sent
to the publication the following information about the "Motto":

> It is the property of the Club, an ever-living re-
> minder, to those of us who follow, of our raison
> d'être. It apotheosizes music's God-given power
> to lift and to alleviate. In it he [Gilchrist] sends
> down through the years his burning words in the
> exaltation of song! The same rare spirit that in-
> spired the Club's inception still resounds in the
> "Motto Song." This song is used as the opening
> number at all our concerts!

Gilchrist's hundredth birthday anniversary was marked
at the May 18, 1946, concert, at which "Cherry Ripe" was
performed. A note on the program told of his many successful years as founder and conductor:

> We honor tonight the memory of the founder of the
> Mendelssohn Club, William Wallace Gilchrist, whose
> hundredth anniversary fell on 8 January, 1946.
>   It was in 1874 that he became Conductor of the
> small group which was the beginning of Mendels-
> sohn Club. Under his capable leadership the Club
> expanded and flourished for thirty-nine years....
> We are happy and proud to pay this tribute to Dr.
> Gilchrist.

The Manuscript Music Society, whose membership included
composers, professional musicians, and associate members,
was founded by Gilchrist in 1891, and its Constitution and
By-Laws were printed in Philadelphia. Article II of the
Constitution stated: "The object of this Society is the ad-
vancement of Musical Composition." Parts of the by-laws
are here quoted to provide an understanding of the organization.

ARTICLE III

Section 1. The Board of Direction, at their first
meeting ... shall elect a Music Committee of three
members, ... two of whom, at least, shall be professional musicians who are composers. The duties
of this committee shall be to pass upon all MSS.
submitted by candidates for membership as composers....
Section 2. The President shall appoint, from the
Board of Direction, a Programme Committee of three
members, chosen from professional musicians. The
duties of this committee shall be to arrange and
supervise all performances given by the Society.

ARTICLE IV

Section 1. Candidates for membership as composers
must submit an original composition, in MS., in any
form they may elect, to the Music Committee of the
Society.... The MS. must not bear the author's
name.... The author's name must not be disclosed
unless the MS. is accepted.... An autograph copy
of the accepted MS. shall become the property of
the Society.
Section 3. Candidates for membership as professional musicians or as associate members must be

> proposed ... by a member of the Society....
> Section 9. It shall be the duty of members to as-
> sist as vocalists or instrumentalists at the private
> concerts of the Society.

Gilchrist was the first president; the other board
members included Hugh A. Clarke, Vice-President (Gilchrist's teacher and professor of music at the University of
Pennsylvania); Philip H. Goepp, Secretary (an organist and
composer); Edward G. McCollin, Treasurer (a singer and
later a founder of the Philadelphia Orchestra, active in the
Musical Fund Society); E.M. Zimmerman, Librarian (a well-
known Philadelphia vocalist); and the Directors, Thomas
A'Becket [junior] (Director of Music at Girard College);
Michael H. Cross (conductor of many choral groups and
teacher); Charles Jarvis (pianist and teacher); and Massah
Warner (organist and composer). These men were all local-
ly well-known professional musicians.

In addition to private concerts and monthly meetings
there were usually two public concerts every year. The
rehearsals and concerts were held at a variety of places in
Philadelphia including the Church of the New Jerusalem,
Witherspoon Hall, Philadelphia Musical Academy and Musical
Fund Hall. The society made use of any facilities that were
available although it did have a definite home during the
1893-1894 and 1894-1895 seasons, an "abiding place suitable
to its purpose and dimensions," as stated in the Report of
the Secretary and of the Treasurer for the year ending
October 3, 1894. The Society, together with the Symphony
Society and Mendelssohn Club, rebuilt the auditorium of the
School of Industrial Arts and for $400 each season had the
use of that room and a smaller room for meetings.

Members were sent letters such as this one from
Charles H. Jarvis, Chairman of the Programme Committee,
to Mr. E.M. Zimmerman on January 19, 1893:

> You are invited to contribute a composition, manu-
> script preferred, for performance at the next
> monthly meeting of the Society.... "At all infor-
> mal musical meetings of the Society, composers
> must be responsible for the performance of their
> works." [extract from Rules of the Board of Di-
> rection].

An early reply, giving the title of the work,
time of performance and name or names of performers is necessary.

Another letter, sent to the members of the Society on October 27, 1893, requested a list of all works available for performance by all members.

The Report of the Secretary for the year ending October 4, 1893, listed a total membership increase from 68 to
113. It also stated that the meetings now had printed programs, the programs always had at least one work of sonata
dimensions, and the first public concert had been held on
May 17 with a full orchestra of fifty. This concert, which
was a financial success, had as its large work William Wallace Gilchrist's Symphony in C major, Number 1.

One of the Society's earliest available programs is
dated November 15, 1893, the second private meeting of the
third season. It reads:

PROGRAMME

1. William W. Gilchrist--
    "Une Petite Suite" for piano, four hands:
    (a) Alla Marcia;
    (b) Melodie;
    (c) Styrienne;
    (d) Fughetta.
2. Hugh A. Clarke (Mus. Doc.)--Songs:
    (a) Spring Love Song
    (b) The Tryst
3. Gustav Hille--Concerto for Violin, No. 4, in
    A major:
    (a) Allegro Moderato;
    (b) Andantino;
    (c) Allegro
4. Alonzo Stone--Songs:
    (a) "Sweetheart"
    (b) "O Sacred Head now wounded"
    (c) "Let the old love come again"
5. Richard Zeckwer--Piano Soli; (a) Etude
    Herman Mohr (b) Traumbilder
                        (c) Perpetuum Mobile
6. Henry A. Lang--Songs:

     (a) "Weist du noch?"

     (b) "Am Wald"

     (c) "Alle Blumen moecht'ich binden"

Gilchrist's Nonet in G minor was also performed during the 1893 season at the December 20 concert. This work, called an outstanding example of nineteenth-century chamber music by Robert Gerson in Music in Philadelphia (Presser, 1940), was chosen many years later for performance in 1975 at the Newport Music Festival. "The Knight of Toggenburg" was performed on April 20, 1898, and his Fantasie for Violin and Piano was praised in an article in The Item (November 21, 1901) as the best work at the November 20, 1901, concert. Other Gilchrist songs and choral works were frequently on the Society's programs.

The Report of the Secretary for the year ending October 3, 1894, provided a list of works produced within that year including Gilchrist's "Fantasy for Organ," probably performed at the February meeting, which was held at the Church of the New Jerusalem; Nonet; and "Une Petite Suite," for piano, four hands.

During the year ending October 1894, the Society had some difficulties. Public interest was declining and contributions had decreased, but by the year's end when the membership increased again the Society was able to hire the auditorium of the School of Industrial Arts. The Report of the Board of Direction for the Season 1895-1896 listed Gilchrist's Quintet for Piano and Strings, performed at the November 20, 1895, concert; A Chorus for Women's Voices; A Cantata for Solos, Chorus and Orchestra (part III); and Three Songs among the Gilchrist works performed during that year. Performance dates were not given in the report, but a program for the November 20 concert exists.

The Trio in G for violin, violoncello, and piano was performed in 1896. The Report of the Board of Direction for the Year Ending October 19, 1898, listed three songs, one ballad and two violin solos among Gilchrist's works performed during the 1897-1898 season. In this report:

     The Board earnestly advise that in future the
     policy of bold advertisement ... be returned or
     even extended.... The Board recommend that in

all concerts of a public or semi-public nature,
there be, if possible, one leader, instead of the
earlier rule, each composer his own conductor
which has a certain disturbing effect upon performers and audience.

In December 1899, Gilchrist wrote in the article "Philadelphia Singing Societies," published in the Musical Courier:

One of the ... unique organizations in Philadelphia
is the Manuscript Society, formed for the purpose
of fostering original composition. It holds monthly
meetings from October to May ... [and] two public
concerts ... each year--one of chamber music and
one of orchestral works. The society is now about
six years old, and in the futherance of its aims
has been remarkably successful.

As membership continued to increase, by the 1908-
1909 season there were 146 members (forty-nine composers,
forty-nine professional musicians and forty-eight associate
members). The January 20, 1909, program still listed Gilchrist as president. The Report of the Board of Direction
that season said:

...there is a continuing need of encouragement of
true composition of the kind that lacks a commercial brand ... it is clear that American composers
need at least the stay and strength that comes
from their own cooperation and from association
with sympathetic music-lovers.... The career of
the Society has been unbroken by deficits or dis-
ruptive episodes....

Gilchrist's Nonet in G minor was performed by the
Hahn Quartette, assisted by members of the Philadelphia Orchestra, at the Society concert on March 17, 1910; a review
in the Public Ledger on March 20, 1910, called the work the
"magnum opus" of the concert. The same group repeated
the Nonet at the Hahn Quartette concert on March 28, 1910.
A Public Ledger article that day praised the work of the
organization:

This society is doing a most important work in giving our own musicians the most practical form of

encouragement, that of enabling their work to be
heard in public under auspicious conditions after
having been submitted to kindly and encouraging
criticism at private rehearsals.

The Nonet in G minor was performed at another Society concert by the same group, the Hahn Quartette, on February
25, 1914. The review in the Public Ledger, February 26,
1914, complimented the work and the Society: "Its mere
existence is a token of the sincere devotion to the cause of
musical culture and the cooperative enthusiasm of Philadelphia musicians."

On May 7, 1914, the Mendelssohn Club and the Manuscript Music Society gave a joint concert. The works were
conducted by the composers who had written them with the
exception of those by Gilchrist, which were led, since Gilchrist was ill, by Herbert Tily, acting conductor of the
Mendelssohn Club.

On November 25, 1914, the Society gave a private
concert and reception for Leopold Stokowski, conductor of
the Philadelphia Orchestra, and Edward W. Bok, one of the
principal contributors to it. Gilchrist's Quintette in F major
was on the program which listed him as the president for
the 1914-1915 season. In 1916 Gilchrist was listed on the
programs as Honorary President and on November 29 that
year the Society presented a concert of all Gilchrist works
as a tribute to him.

I

Fantasy for Violin and Piano Adagio; Allegro;
    Andante

II

Songs   a.   My Ladye
        b.   Sweet is True Love

III

Trio for Piano, Violin and Cello
    Allegro moderato; Scherzo, Allegro molto;
    Adagio; Vivace

IV

Children's Songs a. Meadow Talk
                  b. Little John Bottle John
                  c. Wynken, Blynken and Nod

V

Chorus   a. Charm me asleep
         b. The Fountain

Gilchrist died on December 20, 1916, less than a month after this concert. A Society meeting was held at the Church of the New Jerusalem shortly after he died in order to plan a memorial to the founder, although nothing specific was at that time decided. The society did include some of Gilchrist's music in later programs. On January 23, 1918, at the invitation of the Matinee Music Club, they presented a program which included Gilchrist's Mendelssohn Club "Motto" and "The Day is Gently Sinking to a Close," sung by the Mendelssohn Club, and a solo song, "Descant." On January 11, 1921, at the invitation of the Philadelphia Music Club, the Society presented a Gilchrist Memorial Program arranged by Frances McCollin, a student of Gilchrist's who herself became a Philadelphia composer. The program included choruses for women's voices, "Charm Me Asleep" and "The Bells"; solos for male voice, "Thou'rt like unto a Flow'r" and "Here Awa', There Awa'"; children's songs, "Wynken, Blynken and Nod," "Meadow Talk," "The Gingham Dog and the Calico Cat"; Quintette, Number 1 in C minor for piano and strings.

Concerts given by the Manuscript Music Society were less frequent after Gilchrist died. Philip Goepp, the second "moving spirit" of the organization, died in 1936, and, according to Gerson in Music in Philadelphia (Presser, 1940), the Manuscript Music Society stopped functioning after Goepp's death.

VII. GILCHRIST'S MUSIC

Gilchrist wrote over 250 sacred and secular songs. Although some of them are ordinary, many of the melodies are pleasing, and they are generally free from the excessive sentimentality found in many works of the late romantic period. The poetry Gilchrist used for his songs is sometimes trite, but often he used the works of such poets as Burns and Tennyson, and for many of the sacred works he used biblical texts. For some songs he wrote his own poetry. This line from "Gone Before" expresses the depression he seemed at times to feel: "My soul in sorrow languishes,/Thick darkness is o'er my straying,/And multiplying anguishes...."

The following verse from "Heart's Delight," along with some of his other poetry, was bound into the journal he kept during his trip to Europe in 1886. It was set to music and published the same year.

> Light of my darkness! Star of my night!
> Shedding thy ray o'er my toiling
> Joy of my mourning; O heart's delight,
> Thine is my love, past recalling.
> When thou art grieving, grieveth my heart
> When thou art joying, rejoices!
> When to my loving, loving thou art
> Heavenly music thy voice is--
> Then give thy heart to the heart that is thine,
> Thine only thine, O believe me!
> Dwell not apart, to pity incline
> Open thy heart and receive me--

Rupert Hughes in Contemporary American Composers (L.C. Page, 1900) calls "A Song of Doubt, and a Song of Faith" one of Gilchrist's best compositions. Hughes describes the first part as "a plaint, that is full of cynic despair," and the second as a "cheerful andante." William Treat Upton in Art Song in America (Oliver Ditson, 1930)

describes "the former ["A Song of Doubt"] [as] elaborate--
a veritable scena--full of dramatic color, with a varied and
interesting piano score; the latter ["A Song of Faith"] is
less successful."

"A Song of Doubt" is in three-part song form (ABA).
The A section in c minor has a recitative-like melody with a
skillfully interwoven piano part that enhances the voice
part. [Example 1] A chromatic piano passage [Example 2]
leads to a series of quick modulations which eventually return to c minor and lead into the B section. It is in 3/4
meter with a hymn-like melody, a contrast in mood and meter
to the first part. There is a return to a shortened version
of the A section before the "Song of Faith." This part of
the song, in C major, is simple and not of the same quality
as the first part. [Example 3]

Gilchrist has been compared to other romantic composers. Frederick H. Martins in the Dictionary of American
Biography (1932) states that "in his later songs the influence of Schumann and Franz is sometimes noticeable," and
Upton describes "Nature's Lullaby" as having a "Schumann-
esque texture." [Example 4]

Because Gilchrist deeply loved his children his feeling
was carried over into the many children's songs he composed, such as "Our Country Friends," written as a Christmas present for his daughter, Anna, in 1892. These songs
are usually simple, yet very appealing, as in the effective
setting of Eugene Field's "The Gingham Dog and the Calico
Cat." [Example 5]

The rhythmic patterns in Gilchrist's music are con-
ventional. Common meters are usually employed, and syn-
copation is used sparingly. Sometimes Gilchrist made use of
a 9/8 meter, as in "Heart's Delight," or 6/4, as in "The
New Jerusalem," which also has extended phrases. [Exam-
ple 6] Quick shifts in meter are used infrequently but can
be seen occasionally, as at measure 333 of the "Forty-Sixth
Psalm." [Example 7] The rhythmic pattern for "My Highland
Lassie, O" [Example 8] is also a departure from his usual
figures. Gilchrist employed 6/8 meter in two of his sea
songs, "The Voice of the Sea" and "Waves of the Far Away
Ocean," [Example 9] with sixteenth notes in the piano part
to imitate the motion of ocean waves. Both songs are in g

minor. The melody of "Sing! Sing!" (also in 6/8 meter),
flows in a joyful way, conveying the sentiment of the poetry
by Barry Cornwall. [Example 10] Hughes describes the
rhythm of "Lullaby" as "exquisitely novel." [Example 11]

Gilchrist's melodies for the shorter vocal works usually follow the flow of the words. They are generally four-
measure patterns, repeated with slight variations at the end
or repeated sequentially. Unusual intervals or large jumps
are rarely used. Many melodies move to the top of their
range within the first eight measures, as in "Nature's Lullaby" [Example 12] and "Heart's Delight." [Example 13]
Martins indicates that: "His original compositions ... reflect standard European impacts...." and often exhibit "ly-
ric charm." Sometimes to create a specific effect a melody
will be choppy, but this is a result of the rhythm of the
melody, not the intervals, as in the Scotch song "My Highland Lassie, O." [Example 8, previously quoted] If a song
begins with a recitative section, as in "A Song of Doubt,"
the melody will begin in short detached parts. This also
occurs in "O Lord, Thou Hast Searched Me Out." [Example
14]

In the larger vocal works and instrumental works the
melodic lines are usually developed motivically. A.J. Goodrich in Complete Musical Analysis (John Church, 1889) ex-
trapolates a group of "transformations and elaborations of
the original motive" of the setting of the Forty-Sixth Psalm.
[Example 15] Motivic development can also be seen in the
Symphony in C major. In the second movement the clarinet
introduces this motive. [Example 16] The rhythm is imi-
tated, and the three note ascending figure changed rhythmi-
cally into two sixteenths and a quarter note pattern in the
next motive. [Example 17] The sixteenth notes are incorporated into the next theme [Example 18] which develops into a more elaborate figure. [Example 19] Gilchrist was able
to use this method of motivic development with great facility.
He often used repeated rhythmic patterns in addition to the
melodic designs.

There are no real harmonic surprises in Gilchrist's
music. He made use of traditional harmonic progressions
and cadences in music which has a romantic feeling. His
forms also follow standard modes. Philip Goepp in the Public Ledger, October 24, 1908, writes that:

> Dr. Gilchrist has triumphed over form. Having ac-
> quired the technique he has made himself the mas-
> ter of form and not its servant.... What might
> be a limitation has in his case become a virtue.

His handling of vocal lines and orchestration was not particularly innovative, but he always considered voice ranges
and technical limitations. In the instrumental works he
favored strings and clarinet for introduction of melodic material.

Gilchrist liked to use counterpoint in his compositions.
He sprinkled canonic devices throughout the larger sacred
choral and instrumental works and often included a fugue as
a climax near the end of a movement.

At times he uses word painting; when it occurs it is
of the obvious type such as an ascending line for "flying"
or a descending line for "sighing," seen in measures from
"Joys of Spring," [Example 20] and the sacred song, "O
Lord, Thou Hast Searched Me Out." [Example 21] The
image of Christ rising is represented by ascending lines in
"Christ is Risen," [Example 22] and in "Christ the Lord is
Risen Today." [Example 23]

Gilchrist was probably most creatively inspired as the
composer of sacred choral compositions and sacred songs.
In his long career as a choirmaster he most often used these
genres, and because he was basically a religious person, he
wrote these works easily and effectively.

"O Lord, Thou Hast Searched Me Out" was an extreme-
ly popular sacred song, according to the royalty ledger kept
by Anna Gilchrist. Upton describes it as "a very musician-
ly and effective setting of Psalm 139. If one admit the
legitimacy of dramatic effects in sacred music, this is one
of the very best...." The beginning, in recitative style,
is the section of the melody which employs the most dramatic
effects. [Example 24]

Walter Henry Hall in "William Wallace Gilchrist, An Appreciation," published in the New Music Review (1917),
writes:

> Those who know him only through his songs or

church music, or both, know little about the composer Gilchrist. Most of his songs are graceful,
some of them charming; all his church music is
well written, some of it has distinction. Certain
of his secular choruses, for example "The Uplifted
Gates" and the early cantata "The Rose," are not
only highly effective but also beautiful music. Yet
none of these show the real Gilchrist.

A broad view of the composer's art is seen in such
works as "The Lamb of God," a Passion Oratorio, the
"Christmas Idyll," and the "Easter Idyl." Hall continues:

Here is shown a control of the exigencies of choral
writing, a command of harmonic resources and contrapuntal devices, a gift of melody, and a fluent
invention.... And on occasion there springs up
a fire which shows itself in an unchaining of choral
forces at once thrilling and inspiring. Let the
skeptic examine the final chorus of the "Easter
Idyll [sic]." If he wants sheer beauty let him study
the duet and chorus from the "Passion," "O that my
head were waters."

Gilchrist's setting of the Forty-Sixth Psalm won the
Cincinnati May Festival prize in 1882. A reviewer in the
Cincinnati Commercial, May 20, 1882, felt that its "romantic
beauty ... reminds one of Schumann." Gilchrist himself
wrote a detailed description of the work published in A
Handbook of American Music and Musicians (1887), in which
he states:

My central idea was to make a choral and orchestral work, the solo, while requiring a good singer,
being only secondary. The psalm seemed to me
particularly adapted for musical composition, as
being of varied even dramatic effect.

Gilchrist uses motivic development in this work for orchestra, full chorus, and soprano solo. In a dramatic, effective
treatment of the psalm, he freely uses assorted musical tex-
tures, word-painting and modulation to reflect mood changes.
The final large division of the four-section work includes a
fugue, the subject introduced by bass voices [Example 25],
which is combined with a gloria patri to create a powerful
climactic end.

Most of Gilchrist's instrumental music was performed, but never published. The "Hunting Song" for piano, one of the few published works, is written "in the manner of Mendelssohn, and in it the composer has caught the spirit of the chase," according to William J. Collins, in Laurel Winners: Portraits and Silhouettes of Modern Composers (John Church, 1900). [Example 26] The piano pieces in manuscript are simply constructed, as can be seen in the excerpt from "Joyfulness." [Example 27] The piano accompaniments to the songs usually have more substance than the few solo piano works that Gilchrist wrote.

One of Gilchrist's most interesting pieces of chamber music is the Nonet. Hughes' description of this work reads:

> The Nonet is in G minor, and begins with an Allegro in which a most original and severe subject is developed with infinite grace and an unusually rich color. The Andante is religioso, and is fervent rather than sombre. The ending is especially beautiful. A sprightly Scherzo follows. It is most ingeniously contrived, and the effects are divided with unusual impartiality among the instruments [flute; clarinet; horn; violin I, II; viola; cello; bass; piano]. A curious and elaborate allegro molto furnishes the finale, and ends the Nonet surprisingly with an abrupt major chord.

There are two symphonies among Gilchrist's works for orchestra. Because the full score for the Symphony in D major, Number 2, was lost, only sketches and a reconstructed form of the work exist. The Symphony in C Major, Number 1, was written in 1891. Hughes describes the work as follows:

> The spirit and the treatment ... is strongly classical. While the orchestration is scholarly and mellow, it is not in the least Wagnerian, either in manipulation or in lusciousness. The symphony is not at all programmatic. The Scherzo is of most exuberant gaiety. Its accentuation is much like that in Beethoven's piano sonata (Op. 14, No. 2). Imitation is liberally used in the scoring, with a delightfully comic effect as of an altercation. The symphony ends with a dashing finale that is stormy with cheer.

This symphony, played several times by the Philadelphia Orchestra, in 1901, 1910, 1925, and 1926, always received complimentary reviews. A reviewer for the Philadelphia Press, March 20, 1910, states:

> Instead of putting out a promiscuous assortment of
> melodies loosely interwoven Dr. Gilchrist has pre-
> ferred to work out in various harmonic lines a lim-
> ited number of themes clothed in new form each
> time.... The symphony is genial and cheerful,
> the adagio providing the only shadows....

Although the first symphony was written fourteen years before Gilchrist stopped composing, Hall feels that:

> The climax [of his development] is reached in a
> symphony [Symphony in C major, Number 1]....
> Here are complete mastery of form, rich and spon-
> taneous musical ideas, and an eloquent suggestion
> of what the composer might have done had his daily
> routine of other professional work been less exact-
> ing.

Louis C. Elson, a contemporary of Gilchrist, in The
History of American Music (Macmillan, 1915), believes that
Gilchrist was a strong composer, tied by contrapuntal rules,
who used polyphony with great skill; a well-equipped composer with formal tastes. "In his school [late romantic] he
is the equal of any of our composers and he is ... an un-
questionable home product."

MUSICAL EXAMPLES

Example 1 from "A Song of Doubt"

Example 2 from "A Song of Doubt"

Example 3 from "A Song of Faith"

Example 4 from "Nature's Lullaby"

Example 5 from "The Gingham Dog and the Calico Cat"

Example 6 from "The New Jerusalem"

Example 7 from "The Forty-Sixth Psalm"

NAE GEN-TLE DAMES THOUGH E'ER SAY FAIR SHALL E-VER BE MY MUSE'S CARE

Example 8 from "My Highland Lassie O"

Example 9 from "Waves of the Far Away Ocean"

f SING! SING! MU-SIC WAS GI-VEN TO BRIGHT-EN THE GAY

Example 10 from "Sing! Sing!"

P SOFT-LY IN THE SUM-MER AIR WITH BAL-MY O-DERS LA-DEN

Example 11 from "Lullaby"

SOFT THE DAY-LIGHT IS DE-CLIN-ING ALL THY HO-PING AND RE-PIN-ING TO O-BLIV-ION

Example 12 from "Nature's Lullaby"

TOIL-ING JOY OF MY MOURN-ING O HEART'S DE-LIGHT THINE IS MY LOVE

Example 13 from "Heart's Delight"

O LORD THOU HAST SEARCHED ME OUT   HAST SEARCHED ME OUT AND KNOWN ME

Example 14 from "O Lord, Thou Hast Searched Me Out"

Example 15 from "The Forty-Sixth Psalm"

Example 16 from the Symphony in C Major, number 1

Example 17 from the Symphony in C Major, number 1

Example 18 from the Symphony in C Major, number 1

Example 19 from the Symphony in C Major, number 1

SIGH-ING   TO HER ARMS LET US   FLY   ARMS LET US   FLY

Example 20 from "The Joys of Spring"

AND MY DOWN SIT-TING   IF   I   TAKE   THE   WINGS E-VEN THERE SHALL MY RIGHT HAND UP-HOLD

Example 21 from "O Lord, Thou Hast Searched Me Out"

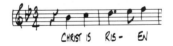

CHRIST IS RIS - EN

Example 22 from "Christ is Risen"

CHRIST THE LORD IS   RIS'N

Example 23 from "Christ the Lord is Risen Today"

(20) POCO AGITATO

IF I   GO UP TO HEAV'N THOU ART   THERE ____   IF I   GO DOWN TO

HELL THOU ART   THERE   IF   I   TAKE   THE   WINGS OF THE MORN-ING

AND   FLY TO THE   END OF THE   EARTH

Example 24 from "O Lord, Thou Hast Searched Me Out"

Example 25 from "The Forty-Sixth Psalm"

Example 26 from "Hunting Song"

Example 27 from "Joyfulness"

EPILOGUE

William Wallace Gilchrist stimulated a great amount of musical activity during his lifetime. He touched the lives of many people both through the groups that he organized and conducted and through his teaching. Because his activities extended beyond Philadelphia the music he published brought his name to people outside the city. Membership in his organizations was large, and members were enthusiastic as were the audiences who came to listen. Gilchrist's choice of repertory elevated the musical taste of his groups and the listeners.

The Manuscript Music Society was especially important because it promoted interest in composition and provided performers and audiences for works that otherwise might never have been heard. The Mendelssohn Club had many loyal members and patrons during Gilchrist's lifetime. They helped to keep the club alive after the death of its founder and maintained the standards that he set. The Mendelssohn Club, still in existence in 1985, is acclaimed as a fine choral group. Gilchrist's work with the Symphony Society aroused enough interest in symphonic music for Philadelphians to establish a permanent professional orchestra in the city.

The testimonials given to Gilchrist confirmed the feelings of love and respect felt by the people who knew him throughout his lifetime. Unfortunately his fame was not as widespread as he would have liked, which was a source of frustration and disappointment to him.

Gilchrist was not innovative as a composer, but his appealing, romantic compositions were always well planned and thoughtfully constructed. Although he tried many types of compositions his best works are the sacred choral compositions such as the inspired setting of the Forty-Sixth Psalm. The fact that he was active as a church composer and choirmaster for many years probably contributed to his

facility in composing sacred works. Gilchrist must have
dreamt of being a great composer, but he did not have the
spark of genius to make him the unique and significant composer he wished to be. His greatness lay in bringing music into the lives of other people.

Gilchrist composing on summer house porch in New England,
c. 1904.

CATALOG CONTENTS

Order of Annotations for Catalog Entries
    Including Abbreviations   71

Terms and Sigla   72

Instrumental
    Symphonic   75
    Ensemble   79
    Keyboard   84

Vocal Works
    Choral Music
        Sacred   88
        Secular   121
    Songs
        Voice and Orchestra   131
        Voice and Keyboard   132

Arrangements   181

Collections
    Children   184
    Hymns   185
    Readers   186
    Vocal Exercises   189

Index of First Lines   191

Order of Annotations for Catalog Entries
Including Abbreviations

1. Number and title

2. Incipit

3. MS: Manuscript information (e.g., Holograph [signed manuscript in composer's hand], Autograph [unsigned manuscript in composer's hand], or manuscript, location, date)

4. Pub: Publication information

5. Parts: or Inst: Parts or instrumentation

6. Text:

7. Ded: Dedicated

8. Ocas.perf: Occasion performed

9. Copy inf: Copyright information (e.g., renewals, included in Catalog of copyright entries)

10. Misc: Miscellaneous information (e.g., included on ARG listing with date, title listed on published song)

11. Agree: Agreements (e.g., material from Presser documents listed in Terms and Sigla)

12. Price: Sale price per copy

13. Royalty rate:

14. Royalties:

15. Perf: Performed

16. Copy: Location of copy

Terms and Sigla

1. **ARG ledger**. Anna R. Gilchrist kept a ledger from 1913 to 1937 with information concerning sale prices, royalty rates, royalty payments and performances for some of her father's music.

2. **ARG listing**. Anna R. Gilchrist began a list of her father's works, probably after he died which is very limited and sometimes incorrect, but does contain some information of value. The listing also makes reference to manuscript books which have not been located and may have been discarded.

3. **Catalog of copyright entries**. Catalog published by Copyright Office of the Library of Congress containing registrations of works entered for copyright.

4. **CNJ**. Church of the New Jerusalem, Philadelphia, Pennsylvania.

5. **Griffin collection**. Collection of Mrs. Margaret Griffin (now deceased), granddaughter of William Wallace Gilchrist. This collection includes the scrapbook; ledger; a journal kept during Gilchrist's European trip containing, among other things, some original poetry; letters; a tribute to Gilchrist from the Musical Fund Society; both a signed manuscript and published copy of "A Maid's Choice"; a copy of Songs for the Children; and a published piano-vocal score of the "Forty-Sixth Psalm."

6. **MC**. Mendelssohn Club of Philadelphia, Pennsylvania.

7. **MS**. Manuscript.

8. **MMS**. Manuscript Music Society of Philadelphia, Pennsylvania.

9. **NUC**. National Union Catalog Pre-1956 Imprints. Listing of works at other libraries with following abbreviations:

CoU	(University of Colorado, Boulder, Colorado)
Cty	(Yale University, New Haven, Connecticut)
CU	(University of California at Berkeley, California)
DLC	(U.S. Library of Congress, District of Columbia)
ICN	(Newberry Library, Chicago, Illinois)
IU	(University of Illinois, Urbana, Illinois)
KMK	(Kansas State University, Manhattan, Kansas)
KU	(University of Kansas, Lawrence, Kansas)
MdBP	(Peabody Institute, Baltimore, Maryland)
MB	(Public Library of the City of Boston, Massachusetts)
MH	(Harvard University, Massachusetts)
MU	(University of Massachusetts in Amherst, Massachusetts)
MiU	(University of Michigan, Ann Arbor, Michigan)
NcD	(Duke University, Durham, North Carolina)
NjP	(Princeton University, Princeton, New Jersey)

NN	(New York Public Library, New York)
NNUT	(Union Theological Seminary, New York)
OCL	(Cleveland Public Library, Ohio)
ODW	(Ohio Wesleyan University, Delaware, Ohio)
OEac	(East Cleveland Public Library, Ohio)
OO	(Oberlin College, Oberlin, Ohio)
OOxM	(Miami University, Oxford, Ohio)
Or	(Oregon State Library, Salem, Oregon)
OrP	(Library Association of Portland, Portland, Oregon)
OrPR	(Reed College, Portland, Oregon)
OrU	(University of Oregon, Eugene)
OU	(Ohio State University, Columbus, Ohio)
PBa	(Academy of the New Church, Bryn Athyn, Pennsylvania)
PP	(Free Library of Philadelphia, Philadelphia, Pennsylvania)
PPL	(Library Company of Philadelphia, Pennsylvania)
PPLT	(Lutheran Theological Seminary, Philadelphia, Pennsylvania)
PPT	(Temple University, Philadelphia, Pennsylvania)
PU	(University of Pennsylvania, Philadelphia, Pennsylvania)
RPB	(Brown University, Providence, Rhode Island)
ViU	(Virginia State Library, Richmond, Virginia)
WaWW	(Whitman College, Wala Wala, Washington)

10. <u>Performance information</u>. This information comes from programs in files and scrapbooks in collections of the Free Library of Philadelphia, the Pennsylvania Historical Society and the ARG ledger. The performances were in Philadelphia unless otherwise noted.

11. <u>Presser documents</u>. Theodore Presser Company in Bryn Mawr, Pennsylvania, has a small file of documents pertaining to William Wallace Gilchrist. The documents are from the Theodore Presser, John Church and Oliver Ditson Companies. They include agreements of sale, certificates of assignment, contracts, copyright certificates, financial statements and letters.

12. <u>Sale price and royalty information</u>. These come from the ARG ledger and Presser documents.

13. <u>SATB</u>. Description of choral music for soprano, alto, tenor, and bass voices.

14. Works of more than one movement are underlined and the name of each movement is in quotation marks.

15. Works of one movement are in quotation marks.

INSTRUMENTAL: SYMPHONIC

1. Suite for Piano and Orchestra

"Scherzo"

"Idyll"

"Rondo Grandiose"

MS: Holograph in Edwin A. Fleisher collection at PP.
Inst: solo piano; flute I, II; oboe I, II; clarinet I, II; bassoon I, II; horn
I, II, III, IV; trombone I, II, III; tuba; tympani; violin I, II; viola; vio-
loncello; bass.

2. "Symphonic Poem"

MS: Holograph in Edwin A. Fleisher collection at PP. Dated by Fleisher
ca. 1910.

Inst: flute I, II; oboe I, II; clarinet I, II; bassoon I, II; horn I, II, III, IV; trumpet I, II; trombone I, II, III; tympani; harp; violin I, II; viola; violoncello; bass.
Perf: MC fortieth anniversary concert, April 14, 1915; Philadelphia Orchestra, April 29, 30, 1921, for unveiling of Gilchrist bas-relief; Civic Symphony Orchestra (W.P.A. Federal Music Project), February 7, 1937.

3. Symphony in C major, Number 1

"Vivace Impetuoso"

"Adagio"

"Scherzo"

"Finale"

MS: MS by copyist in Edwin A. Fleisher collection at PP. Dated 1891 by Fleisher. Holograph of four hand arrangement in collection of PP.
Inst: piccolo; flute I, II; oboe I, II; clarinet I, II; bassoon I, II; horn I, II, III, IV; trumpet I, II; trombone I, II, III; tuba; tympani; violin I, II; viola; violoncello; bass.
Perf: Symphony Society and MMS joint concert, May 17, 1892; Philadelphia Orchestra: February 8, 9, 1901; March 4, 5, 1910; December 18, 1925; August 30, 1926; Civic Symphony Orchestra (W.P.A. Federal Music Project), February 20, 1938; Chestnut Hill Symphony Orchestra, November 1975; Old York Road Symphony Orchestra, April 1982.

4. Symphony in D major, Number 2

"Allegro Moderato"

"Contemplative"

"Finale--Allegro"

MS: Combination autograph and MS by William F. Happich (sketches for symphony were edited and completed by Happich in 1933, full score was lost) in collection of PP.
Inst: flute I, II; oboe I, II; clarinet I, II; bassoon I, II; horn I, II, III, IV; trumpet I, II; trombone I, II, III; tuba; tympani; percussion; harp, violin I, II; viola; violoncello; bass.
Perf: Symphony Club, April 13, 1933; Civic Symphony Orchestra (W.P.A. Federal Music Project), April 9, 1937.

5. Symphonic Sketches

"Intermezzo"

MS: Autograph in collection of PP.
Inst: flute; clarinet; bassoon I, II; horn; violin I, II; viola; violoncello; bass.
Misc: MS was reviewed by William F. Happich in 1933. Note by Happich on score:

> Composed previous to the 2nd Symphony. This number was prob-
> ably the inspiration or originating point for the symphony. Dr. Gil-
> christ probably intended to use this number in the symphony, but
> abandoned the idea when he evolved a different plan and it did not
> fit in very well with the new conception.

6. "I. '?' and II. 'Solenell'"

I. '?'

II. Solenell

<u>MS</u>:   Autograph in collection of PP.
<u>Inst</u>:   flute I, II; oboe; clarinet; bassoon; trumpet I, II; horn I, II; trombone I, II; tuba; tympani; violin I, II; viola; violoncello; bass.
<u>Misc</u>:   MS was reviewed by William F. Happich in 1933. Notes by Happich on score:

> Two fragments of compositions which have no bearing at all on the Symphony [in D major, Number 2]. It seems evident that these are from a much earlier date.

INSTRUMENTAL: ENSEMBLE

7. Fantasie for Violin and Piano

"Introduction: Adagio"

"Allegro con abandon"

"Andante espressivo"

MS: Holograph in collection of PP.
Ded: to E.I. Keffer.
Perf: MMS, January 16, 1895; Melody Club, April 27, 1899; MSS, November 20, 1901, November 29, 1916; Art Alliance 1937.

8. Nonet in G minor

"Allegro"

"Adagio religioso"

"Scherzo"

"Finale"

MS: Holographs in collection of PP for piano, instrumental score and eight parts. ARG listing, 1890s.
Inst: piano, flute, clarinet, horn, string quintette (violin I, II; viola; violoncello; bass).
Perf: Hahn Quartette, March 28, 1910; Newport Music Festival, August 1975.

9. "Novelette"

MS: Holograph in collection of PP for piano-violin score and violin part.

10. Quintette in C minor, Number 1

"Allegro"

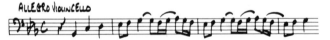

"Scherzo"

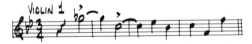

"Adagio"

"Allegro"

MS: Holographs in collection of PP for string parts only. ARG listing,
1890s.
Inst: violin I, II; viola; violoncello; piano.
Ded: M.N. Warner.
Perf: MMS first private meeting 1892, November 20, 1895; New Century
Drawing Room, February 16, 1898; MMS, December 19, 1917; Gilchrist
Memorial Program, January 11, 1921.

11. Quintette in F major, Number 2

"Allegro spiritoso"

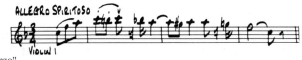

"Scherzo"

"Andante"

"Molto Moderato--Maestoso"

MS: Photocopy of manuscript edition by Charlton Louis Murphy dated January 1943 in collection of PP. ARG listing, late work, notation on listing,
"This quintette finished while he was sick, or possibly not finished to his
satisfaction. Apparently written 20 years after c minor."
Perf: MMS, March 25, 1914; Matinee Musical, March 31, 1914; University
of Pennsylvania Alumnae Concert, May 21, 1914; MMS, November 23, 1914,
December 18, 1914; Galen Hall, Atlantic City, New Jersey, January 1,
1915; Society of Arts and Letters, November 19, 1915; Hahn School, December 14, 1915; de Pasquale String Quartet with Sylvia Glickman at Haverford College, Haverford, Pennsylvania, January 25, 1976.

12. "Rhapsodie"

Inst: violin and piano.
Perf: MMS, May 8, 1899.

13. Suite for Violin and Piano, Number 1

"Reverie"

"Intermezzo"

"Perpetual Motion"

MS: Holographs in collection of PP for piano-violin score and violin part.
Perf: MMS, May 18, 1899; Melody Club, April 13, 1903.

14. Suite for Violin and Piano, Number 2

"Ballade"

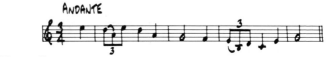

"Hymnus"

"Scherzo"

MS: Holographs in collection of PP for piano-violin score and violin part.

15. Suite for Piano and Violoncello

Misc: Three movements: "Scherzo"; "Melodia continua"; "Rondo grandioso."
Perf: MMS, March 22, 1911.

16. Trio in G minor

"Allegro moderato"

"Scherzo"

"Adagio"

<u>MS</u>: Autograph in collection of PP. ARG listing, early work.
<u>Ded</u>: to Richard Zeckwer.
<u>Perf</u>: Grand Testimonial Concert in honor of William Wallace Gilchrist,
January 15, 1886; MMS, January 27, 1897; Melody Club, April 21, 1904;
MMS, November 29, 1916.

17. "Allegretto"

Inst: Piano.
Perf: MMS, October 17, 1894.
Copy: MB (listed in catalog of Allen A. Brown Collection as "Autograph manuscript. [1894.]").

18. "Allegro"

MS: Autograph in collection of PP.
Inst: Piano.

19. "Andante"

Pub: Vox organi. Boston: J.B. Millet Co., 1896, volume IV. Music for organ.
Copy: DLC, MB (listed in catalog of Allen A. Brown collection as "Autograph manuscript. [189-?]").

20. "Andante expressivo"

MS: Autograph in collection of PP.
Inst: Piano.

21. "Duetto"

MS: Autograph in collection of PP.
Inst: Piano (another part indicated at times on score).

22. Fantasia in D minor for Organ

Misc: Four movements: "Adagio maestoso"; "Allegro moderato"; "Andante
con expressive"; "Allegro."
Perf: Organ Recital #56, under auspices of American Organ Players Club,
March 31, 1894.

23. "Hunting Song"

Pub: Cincinnati: John Church, 1894.
Inst: Piano.
Copy: DLC.

24. "Maid's Choice, A"

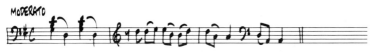

MS: Holograph in Griffin collection.
Pub: Harper's Magazine, December 1891.
Inst: Musical pastoral for piano, illustrated, with narrative.
Copy: Griffin collection (published copy and holograph), MdBP, PP.

25. Petite Suite, Une

1. "Alla Marcia"

2. "Melodie"

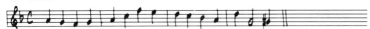

3. "Styrienne"

4. "Fughetta"

MS: Manuscript in collection of DLC (complete).
Pub: Boston: Arthur P. Schmidt, 1885.
Inst: Piano, four hands.
Perf: MMS, November 15, 1893; "Alla Marcia," "Melodie," "Syrienne" per-
formed Polyhymnia Choral, January 29, 1894.
Copy: LC incomplete, 3. "Styrienne" missing.

26. Prelude and Fugue in G minor

Inst: Piano.
Misc: ARG listing, 1890, dedicated to Charley.
Perf: MMS, October 17, 1894.

27. "Romanza"

Pub: Famous Composers and Their Music. Boston: J.B. Millet Co., 1901.
Perf: Melody Club, April 29, 1897.

28. Sonata for Organ

Misc: ARG listing, published by J.B. Millet, Boston, 1896. Three movements: "Andante"; "Sonata"; "Fantasy."

29. Sonata for Organ in D

Misc: Three movements: "Introduction--Allegro"; "Andante"; "Intermezzo
--Fugue."
Perf: MMS, February 15, 1893.

30. Three Pieces for Pianoforte

"Scherzo"

"Berceuse"

"Nocturne"

MS: Holograph in collection of PP.
Perf: "Berceuse," MMS, October 17, 1894.

31. Two Short Pieces for Piano

"Meditation"

"Joyfulness"

MS: Holograph in collection of PP.

32. "Waltz for Piano"

Misc: ARG listing.

VOCAL: CHORAL MUSIC (SACRED)

33. "All Things So Bright and Beautiful"

Pub: New Hosanna. New York: New Church Board of Publication, 1902.
Hosanna. New York: New Church Press, 1920. Hosanna. revised edi-
tion. Boston: The Swedenborg Press, 1968.
Text: Mrs. C.F. Alexander.
Ocas. perf: Flower Day.
Copy: CNJ (Hosanna 1920, 1968), PBa (New Hosanna)

34. "Angels Roll the Stone Away"

MS: MS by copyist in collection of PP. Three copies of part one, three
copies of part two, two copies part three, and piano part. Easter 1898.
Parts: Trio for female voices.
Text: [Thomas Scott.] Notes on MS "For Woodland Church," "Chorus--
Easter April 10, 1898."

35. "Arlington Communion"

Pub: Magnificat. New York: New Church Board of Publication, 1910.
Copy: CNJ.

36. "Aspiration"

Pub: Presbyterian Hymnal. Philadelphia: Presbyterian Board of Public
and Sabbath School Work, 1895.
Copy: DLC.

37. "Ave Maria"

<u>Pub</u>: Philadelphia: William Wallace Gilchrist.
<u>Parts</u>: Double chorus, piano and organ.
<u>Misc</u>: Entered in Catalog of Copyright Entries, February 12, 1890.
<u>Perf</u>: MMS, March 24, 1897, May 13, 1897; MC and MMS, May 7, 1914.

38. "Behold My Servant"

<u>Pub</u>: New York: G. Schirmer, 1894.
<u>Parts</u>: Four parts, may be sung by all male voices with keyboard.
<u>Text</u>: from Isaiah.
<u>Ocas. perf</u>: Christmas anthem.
<u>Copy</u>: DLC.

39. "Behold Now, Fear Ye Not"

<u>Pub</u>: New York: G. Schirmer, 1894.
<u>Parts</u>: SATB with soprano, solo, and organ.
<u>Text</u>: from Gospels and Prophecies.
<u>Ded</u>: Mr. Arthur D. Woodruff, New York.
<u>Perf</u>: CNJ, April 21, 1946.
<u>Copy</u>: DLC.

40. "Belfield"

<u>Pub</u>: Presbyterian Hymnal. Philadelphia: Presbyterian Board of Public
and Sabbath School Work, 1895.
<u>Text</u>: Isaac Watts.
<u>Copy</u>: DLC.

41. "Benedic Anima (in G)"

<u>Pub</u>: New York: G. Schirmer, 1883.
<u>Copy inf</u>: Copyright renewed 1911.
<u>Price</u>: $.25.
<u>Royalty rate</u>: 10 percent.

42. "Benedictus (F major)"

<u>Misc</u>: ARG listing.

43. "Benedictus (G major)"

<u>Misc</u>: ARG listing.

44. "Bethlehem"

<u>Pub</u>: Cincinnati: John Church Co., 1898.
<u>Parts</u>: SATB and soprano solo with organ.
<u>Text</u>: Phillips Brooks.
<u>Ocas. perf</u>: Christmas.
<u>Agree</u>: Assigned to John Church, April 20, 1898 for $40 with three other works. (Presser Documents. Other works were "All My Heart this Day Rejoices," "From Heaven Above," "Once in Royal David's City.")
<u>Copy</u>: DLC.

45. "Bless the Lord, O My Soul"

<u>MS</u>: Holograph in collection of PP.
<u>Parts</u>: SATB (called "quartett" on MS) and keyboard.
<u>Text</u>: from Psalm 103.

46. "Blessed Night"

<u>Pub</u>: <u>Presbyterian Hymnal</u>. Philadelphia: Presbyterian Board of Public and Sabbath School Work, 1895.
<u>Text</u>: Horatius Bonar.
<u>Copy</u>: DLC.

47. "Blow on, Thou Mighty Wind"

<u>Parts</u>: Hymn for choir.
<u>Perf</u>: MMS, June 7, 1905.

48. "Boner"

IN - SPIRER   AND HEAR- ER   OF -   PRAYER

Pub: Book of Common Praise. Philadelphia: Reformed Episcopal Publication Society, 1885.
Copy: PP.

49. "Bonum Est"

Pub: New York: G. Schirmer, 1883.
Parts: Quartett or chorus.
Copy inf: Copyright renewed January 1911.
Price: $.15.
Royalty rate: 10 percent.

50. "Calm on the List'ning Ear of Night"

CALM ON THE LIS-TE-NING EAR OF NIGHT

Pub: New York: G. Schirmer, 1889.
Parts: SATB and soprano solo with organ.
Text: Edmund H. Sears.
Ded: Bertha B. Goodman, Philadelphia.
Ocas. perf: Christmas.
Copy inf: Copyright renewed 1917 by Anna R. Gilchrist.
Copy: DLC.

51. "Cantate Domino (G major, Number one)"

Pub: New York: G. Schirmer, 1883.
Copy inf: Copyright renewed January 1911.
Price: $.11.

52. "Cantate Domino (G major, Number two)"

Misc: ARG listing.

53. "Cary"

ONE SWEETLY SOLEMN   THOUGHT

Pub: Presbyterian Hymnal. Philadelphia: Presbyterian Board of Public
and Sabbath School Work, 1895.

Text: Phoebe Cary.
Copy: DLC.

54. "Children Can You Tell"

Pub: Hosanna. New York: New Church Press, 1920.
Copy: CNJ.

55. "Christ Church"

Pub: Book of Common Praise. Philadelphia: Reformed Episcopal Publication Society, 1885.
Copy: PP.

56. "Christ is Risen"

Pub: Philadelphia: William H. Boner, 1877.
Parts: SATB with keyboard.
Ocas. perf: Easter anthem.
Copy: DLC, PP.

57. "Christ our Passover"

Pub: Philadelphia: William H. Boner, 1879.
Parts: SATB with organ.
Ocas. perf: Eastern anthem.
Copy: DLC.

58. "Christ our Passover"

Pub: New York: G. Schirmer, 1883.
Parts: SATB with organ.
Ocas. perf: Easter anthem.
Copy inf: Copyright renewed 1911.
Copy: LC.

59. "Christ our Passover"

Pub: New York: G. Schirmer, 1887.
Parts: SATB.
Ocas. perf: Easter anthem.
Copy inf: Copyright renewed 1915.
Price: $.25.
Royalty rate: 10 percent.
Royalties: February 1926, $12.50; February 1927, 25 copies sold for 6.25;
1929, 24 copies sold for 6.00; February 1930, 24 copies sold for 6.00; 1932,
20 copies sold, royalty .50.
Copy: DLC.

60. "Christ the Lord is Risen Today"

Pub: New York: G. Schirmer, 1886.
Parts: SATB with soprano solo and organ.
Text: Michael Weiss.
Ocas. perf: Easter hymn.
Copy: DLC.

61. "Christians Awake"

Pub: New York: G. Schirmer, 1886.
Parts: Women's voices and organ.
Ocas. perf: Christmas anthem.
Copy inf: Copyright renewed 1914.
Perf: MC, December 10, 1914.

62. Christmas Idyll, A

I. "Desolation"

II. "Promise"

III. "Fulfillment"

Pub: Boston: Oliver Ditson Co., 1894.
Parts: SATB and solos with orchestra; SATB and solos with piano reduction.
Text: from the Scriptures.
Misc: ARG listing, "plates given to Presser 1911 and MS parts for full orchestra and score left with Presser, 1931."
Price: $1.00
Royalty rate: 10 percent.
Royalties: October 1914, $1.30; October 1915, 2.40; October 1917, 1.00; October 1918, 2.60; October 1919, 2.80; October 1921, 4.90; April 1923, 1.30; October 1923, 4.20; April 1925, 4.70; October 1926, 1.60; October 1928, 2.10; April 1934, 1.76; October 1934, 3.60; October 1935, 2.30; March 1935, 1.12; March 1936, 1.38.
Copy: NN (piano-vocal score).

63. "Christmas Service for Sunday School"

Misc: ARG listing. Title listed on "O Many and Many a Year Ago," published by G. Schirmer, New York.

64. "Come Gracious Spirit"

Misc: ARG listing, published by G. Schirmer, New York.
Royalty rate: $.08 per copy, 10 percent of sale price.
Royalties: February 1913, $1.05; 1914, .48; 1915, .54; 1917, .62; 1918, .43; February 1921, .80; February 1924, .80; February 1925, 1.04; February 1928, .80; February 1927, 50 copies sold, 4.00; February 1928, 100 copies sold, 8.00; 1929, 150 copies sold, 12.00; February 1930, 4.00; February 1931, 12.00; 1933, 10 copies sold, .80.

65. "Come See the Place Where Jesus Lay"

Pub: Philadelphia: William Wallace Gilchrist, 1887; Cincinnati: John Church Co., 1895.
Parts: SATB and soprano solo with keyboard.

Text: [Richard Crashaw.]
Ocas. perf: Easter.
Copy inf: Copyright renewed 1915.
Agree: Assigned to John Church Co., February 16, 1894 for $50, with two
other works. (Presser Documents. Other works were "Hunting Song,"
"The Sun and the Rosebud.")
Copy: DLC.

66. "Confidence"

Pub: Magnificat. New York: New Church Board of Publication, 1910.
Text: from Psalm 46.
Copy: CNJ.

67. "Dager"

Pub: Book of Common Praise. Philadelphia: Reformed Episcopal Publication Society, 1885.
Copy: PP.

68. "Day is Gently Sinking, The"

Pub: New York: G. Schirmer, 1886.
Parts: SATB and baritone solo with keyboard.
Text: Saint Anatolius.
Copy inf: Copyright renewed 1914, 1942.
Misc: ARG listing notation, "Sung at Pa's funeral by MC and played at
Ma's by organist."
Perf: MMS, January 23, 1918.
Copy: DLC.

69. "Day is Past and Over, The"

Pub: Boston: Oliver Ditson, 1914.
Parts: SATB with solo and organ.
Text: Saint Anatolius and J.M. Neale.
Agree: Agreement for 10 percent royalty October 1913. (Presser Documents.)
Price: $.12.
Copy: DLC, PP.

70. "De Profundis"

MS: Holograph in collection of PP dated September 20, 1883, New London, Pa.
Parts: SATB and orchestra (flute; oboe; clarinet; bassoon; trumpet, horn I, II; tenor trombone I, II; bass trombone; tuba; violin I, II; viola; violoncello; bass).
Text: from Psalm 130.

71. "Deus Misereatur (F major)"

Pub: New York: G. Schirmer, 1883.
Copy inf: Copyright renewed 1911.
Price: $.20。
Royalties: February 1922, $1.00.

72. "Dominus regit me (Psalm 22)"

MS: Holograph in collection of PP.
Parts: Soprano, alto and bass voices.
Misc: Note on MS, "Adaptation de paroles latines par G. Couture."

73. "Easter Idyl"

MS: Autograph in collection of PP.
Parts: Chorus I, SATB; Chorus II, SATB; orchestra (flute I, II; oboe I, II; clarinet I, II; bassoon I, II; horn I, II; trombone I, II; violin I, II; viola; violoncello; bass; organ).
Pub: New York: G. Schirmer, 1907.
Parts: SATB with piano.
Text: Selected from Scriptures with hymn by Frank Sewell.
Price: $.75.

Royalties: 1914, $.15; 1916, .23; February 1923, 2.85; February 1924,
.90; February 1926, 5.18; February 1927, 71 copies sold, 53.25; February
1928, 45 copies sold, 33.75; 1929, 3 copies sold, 2.25; February 1930,
10.50; February 1931, 5.25; February 1932, 2 copies sold, .15; March
1933, .07.
Perf: MC, April 18, 1907.
Copy: LC (piano-vocal score).

74. "Emmanuel"

Pub: Boston: Oliver Ditson, 1898.
Parts: SATB with organ.
Text: William C. Dix.
Ocas. perf: Christmas.
Price: $.16.
Royalties: July 1929, $1.36; July 1931, .15; July 1932, .45; July 1933,
.56.
Copy: DLC.

75. "Except the Lord Build the House"

Pub: New York: G. Schirmer, 1886.
Parts: SATB with organ.
Text: from Psalm 127.
Ocas. perf: Anthem for dedication or consecration.
copy inf: Copyright renewed 1914.
Copy: DLC.

76. "Father of All"

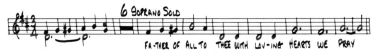

Pub: New York: Charles S. Elliot and Co., 1897.
Parts: SATB and keyboard.
Text: John Julian
Price: $.10.
Copy: DLC.

98   William Wallace Gilchrist

77. "Festum Dei"

O BREAD TO PIL- GRIMS GIV — EN

Pub: Presbyterian Hymnal. Philadelphia: Presbyterian Board of Public
and Sabbath School Work, 1895.
Text: Latin ca. seventeenth century, anonymous.
Copy: DLC.

78. "Forsake Me Not"

FOR - SAKE ME NOT

Pub: Magnificat. New York: New Church Board of Publication, 1910;
Book of Worship. New York: New Church Board of Publication, 1950.
Copy: CNJ (both books).

79. "Forty-sixth Psalm, The"[1]

ANDANTE CONTEMPLATIF

156 SOPRANO

GOD IS OUR RE-FUGE AND STRENGTH

MS: Autograph in collection of PP dated August 21, 1881.
Parts: Orchestra score (flute I, II; oboe I, II; clarinet I, II; bassoon I,
II; horn I, II, III, IV; trombone; tympani, G, D; violin I, II; viola; violon-
cello, bass).
Misc: Notation on cover, "published by Schirmer, 1882," "Time of Per-
formance 35-45 minutes."
Pub: New York: G. Schirmer, 1882.
Parts: SATB and soprano solo with orchestra; SATB and soprano solo
with piano reduction.
Misc: Prize composition of the Cincinnati Music Festival, 1882.
Copy: Griffin Collection, ICN, MB, MiU, NN, NjP, PPL, PPLT, of Boston.

80. "From the Holy Heaven"

FROM THE HO - LY HEA - VEN

Pub: Hosanna for Children. New York: New Church Board of Publication, 1905.
Copy: CNJ.

---

[1]Listed as "God is our Refuge and Strength" in NUC and catalog of Public Library of the City of Boston.

81. "Glad Day"

HE HAS COME THE CHRIST OF GOD

Pub: Presbyterian Hymnal. Philadelphia: Presbyterian Board of Public
and Sabbath School Work, 1895.
Text: Horatius Bonar.
Copy: DLC.

82. "Gloria in Excelsis (F major)"

GLORY BE TO LORD HEAVENLY KING

Pub: Philadelphia: William Wallace Gilchrist, 1888. Magnificat. New York:
New Church Board of Publication, 1910; Book of Worship. New York: New
Church Board of Publication, 1968.
Parts: SATB and organ.
Copy inf: Copyright renewed 1916.
Copy: CNJ (both books).

83. "Gloria in Excelsis (G major)"

Pub: Philadelphia: William Wallace Gilchrist, 1883.
Copy inf: Copyright renewed 1911.
Price: $.15.
Royalty rate: 10 percent.
Royalties: February 1924, $.75.

84. "Gloria in Excelsis (for ordinary use, in C major)"

Pub: New York: G. Schirmer, 1889.
Copy inf: Copyright renewed 1917 by Anna R. Gilchrist.

85. "God is my Strong Salvation"

ALLEGRO

GOD IS MY STRONG SAL - VA - TION

Pub: New York: G. Schirmer, 1905.
Parts: SATB with tenor solo and organ.
Text: James Montgomery.
Copy inf: Copyright renewed 1933.
Price: $.15.
Royalty rate: 10 percent.
Royalties: February 1913, $2.28; 1914, 1.72; 1915, .69; 1916, 1.38; 1917,
2.05; 1918, .60; 1919, 1.50; February 1921, 2.25; February 1922, 1.73;
February 1923, 1.04; February 1925, 1.95; February 1926, 2.77; February

1927, 50 copies sold for 7.50; February 1928, 50 copies sold for 7.50;
February 1932, 54 copies, .81 royalty.
Copy: DLC.

86. "God that Madest Earth and Heaven"

Pub: New York: G. Schirmer, 1892.
Parts: Quartette or chorus and soprano solo with organ.
Text: [Reginald Heber.]
Perf: MMS, March 24, 1897.
Copy: DLC.

87. "Greeting"

Pub: Magnificat. New York: New Church Board of Publication, 1910.
Text: James Montgomery.
Copy: CNJ.

88. "Hark, What Mean Those Holy Voices"

Pub: New York: G. Schirmer, 1895.
Parts: SATB and soprano solo with organ.
Text: J. Cawood.
Ocas. perf: Christmas.
Copy inf: Copyright renewed 1923 by Anna R. Gilchrist.
Copy: DLC.

89. "He is Risen"

Copy inf: Entered in the Catalog of Copyright Entries, December 14,
1886. Copyright renewed 1914.
Misc: Title listed on "Magnificat in G" published by G. Schirmer.

90. "Hide Me O Twilight Air"

Pub: New York: G. Schirmer, 1910.
Parts: SATB with four hand accompaniment.
Text: Barry Cornwall.
Copy inf: Copyright renewed 1938.

Misc: ARG listing notations, "Sung In Memoriam for 'Ma' by MC," 1873 MS
book.

91. "Hoffman"

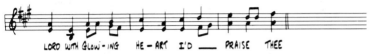

LORD WITH GLOW-ING   HE-ART I'D ___ PRAISE THEE

Pub: Book of Common Praise. Philadelphia: Reformed Episcopal Publication Society, 1895.
Copy: PP.

92. "Holy Night"

Misc: ARG listing, Easter hymn.

93. "Hopkins"[2]

BLOW ON THE MIGH-TY   WIND ___

Pub: Book of Common Praise. Philadelphia: Reformed Episcopal Publica-
tion Society, 1885.
Text: J.H. Hopkins.
Copy: PP.

94. "Hosanna, Loud Hosanna"

HO - SAN - NA LOUD HO - SAN - NA

Pub: New Hosanna. New York: New Church Board of Publication, 1902;
Hosanna. New York: New Church Press, 1920.
Copy: CNJ (Hosanna), PBa (New Hosanna).

95. "How long wilt Thou forget me, O Lord"

ADAGIO SOLENELLE

HOW LONG WILT THOU FOR-GET ME O LORD

MS: Autograph in collection of PP.
Parts: SATB and contralto solo with organ.
Text: Psalm 12.
Perf: MMS, January 19, 1898.

---
[2]Published as "Whitsuntide," in Magnificat. See p. 120.

96. "I Heard the Voice of Jesus Say"

Pub: New York: G. Schirmer, 1909.
Parts: SATB or quartet and tenor solo with organ.
Text: Horatius Bonar.
Copy inf: Copyright renewed 1936.
Price: $.12.
Royalty rate: 10 percent.
Royalties: February 1913, $3.54; 1914, .48; 1915, 6.81; 1916, 3.05; 1917, 3.53; 1918, 1.60; 1919, 3.40; February 1921, 4.80; February 1922, 5.82; February 1923, 4.20; February 1924, 8.14; February 1925, 4.80; February 1926, 6.90; February 1927, 300 copies sold for 36.00; February 1928, 275 copies sold for 33.12; 1929, 249 copies sold for 28.88. February 1930, 35.88; February 1931, 18.00; February 1932, 134 copies sold, 1.61; March 1933, 1.80.
Copy: DLC.

97. "I Love My God"

Misc: ARG listing, published by William H. Boner, Philadelphia, 1883.

98. "I Love Thee Lord"

Pub: New York: E.S. Lorenz, 1900.
Parts: SATB and soprano solo with keyboard.
Text: [Connie Calenberg.]
Copy: DLC.

99. "I Will Lift Up My Eyes (Psalm 121)"

Pub: New York: G. Schirmer, 1889.
Parts: Trio or three part chorus for women's voices with piano.
Copy inf: Copyright renewed 1917 by Anna R. Gilchrist.
Perf: MMS, April 22, 1896.
Copy: DLC.

100. "If ye then be ris'n with Christ"

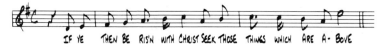

MS: Holograph in collection of PP.
Parts: SATB with organ.
Text: from Psalm 57.
Ocas. perf: Easter.
Perf: CNJ, Easter service April 16, 1911.

101. "In the Beginning Was the Word"

MS: Holograph in collection of PP.
Parts: Soprano and organ.
Pub: Cincinnati: John Church Co., 1901.
Parts: SATB with keyboard.
Text: from Saint John I.
Ocas. perf: Christmas.
Copy inf: Copyright renewed 1929.
Agree: Assigned to John Church Co., October 4, 1900 for $25. (Presser Documents.)
Misc: Notes on MS, "Hymn for Christmas," "Publisher--John Church 1901."
Copy: DLC, NN.

102. "It Came Upon a Midnight Clear"

Pub: New York: G. Schirmer, 1886.
Parts: SATB with organ.
Text: Edmund Hamilton Sears.
Ocas. perf: Christmas.
Copy inf: Copyright renewed 1914.
Perf: MC, December 10, 1914.
Copy: DLC.

103. "It Came Upon a Midnight Clear"

Pub: New Hosanna. New York: New Church Board of Publication, 1902.
Text: Rev. E.H. Sears.
Copy: PBa.

104. "Jesus, I My Cross Have Taken"

Pub: Boston: Oliver Ditson, 1905. Our Sweetest Music [n.p.]: William
S. Whiteford, 1901.
Parts: SATB and organ.
Text: Henry F. Lyte.
Misc: Entered in Catalog of Copyright Entries November 24, 1882.
Price: $.12.
Copy: DLC.

105. "Jesus, Lover of My Soul"

Pub: New York: G. Schirmer, 1903.
Parts: SATB and soprano solo with organ.
Text: Charles Wesley.
Price: $.15.
Royalty rate: 10 percent.
Royalties: February 1913, .51; 1914, .68; 1916, .20; February 1927, 39
copies sold for 5.85; February 1930, 59 copies sold for 8.85.
Copy: DLC.

106. "Jesus Loves Me"

Pub: Hosanna for Children. New York: New Church Board of Publication, 1905.
Copy: CNJ.

107. "Jesus, the Very Thought of Thee"

Pub: New York: G. Schirmer, 1892.
Parts: SATB or quartet and alto solo with organ.
Text: attributed to Saint Bernard of Clairvaux.
Copy: DLC.

108. "Jubilate Deo (A^b major)"

Misc: Title listed on "Sweet Saviour Bless Us Ere We Go," published by
G. Schirmer, New York.

109. "Jubilate Deo (B^b major)"

Pub: New York: G. Schirmer, 1886.
Parts: SATB.
Copy inf: Copyright renewed 1914.

110. "Jubilate Deo (C major)"

Misc: ARG listing.

111. "Jubilate Deo (F major)"

Misc: ARG listing.
Price: $.10.

112. "Jubilate Deo (G major)"

Copy inf: Copyright renewed 1908, 1921 by Mrs. William Wallace [Susan
B.] Gilchrist.

113. "Just As I Am"

Pub: New York: G. Schirmer, 1905.
Parts: SATB chorus or quartet and soli with organ.
Copy inf: Copyright renewed 1932 by Anna R. Gilchrist.
Perf: MMS, June 7, 1905.
Copy: DLC.

114. "Kyrie"

Pub: Magnificat. New York: New Church Board of Publication, 1910.
Copy: CNJ.

115. "Lamb of God"

Pub: New York: H.W. Gray Co., 1909.
Parts: SATB and reader with organ.
Text: James Montgomery.
Misc: ARG listing, orchestra parts in MS with Gray to rent for $10.
Perf: CNJ, April 1908, 1909; Cathedral of Saint John the Divine, New
York, April 1, 1909; Columbia University Chapel, New York, March 21,
1917; First Presbyterian Church, Philadelphia, April 1925; Walnut Street
Presbyterian Church, Philadelphia, April 1933; Second Presbyterian Church,
Philadelphia, 1946.
Copy: DLC, ICN, MiU.

116. "Laudate"

MS: MS by copyist in collection of PP.
Parts: voice parts only, no score; 8 parts for soprano; 4 for alto (4, 6,
7, 8 missing); 8 for tenor; 7 for bass (3 missing).

117. "Light of the World"

Pub: Presbyterian Hymnal. Philadelphia: Presbyterian Board of Public
and Sabbath School Work, 1895.
Text: John S.B. Monsell.
Copy: DLC.

118. "Like as a Father"

Pub: New York: G. Schirmer, 1886.
Parts: Trio for alto, tenor, baritone and piano.
Copy inf: Copyright renewed 1914.
Copy: DLC.

119. "Lord Reigneth, The"

<u>Pub</u>: New York: E.S. Lorenz, 1900.
<u>Parts</u>: SATB and keyboard.
<u>Ocas. perf</u>: Thanksgiving.

120. "Lord, What is Man"

LORD WHAT IS MAN THAT THOU ART MIND — FUL OF HIM

<u>MS</u>: Holograph in collection of PP.
<u>Parts</u>: SATB
<u>Text</u>: Psalm text.

121. "Lord, With a Glowing Heart I'd Praise Thee"

<u>Misc</u>: ARG listing, published by Oliver Ditson, Boston, 1892.
<u>Price</u>: $.16.

122. "Magnificat (F major)"

<u>Pub</u>: Philadelphia: William Wallace Gilchrist, 1887.
<u>Copy inf</u>: Copyright renewed 1915.

123. "Magnificat (G major, Festival)"

MY SOUL DOTH MAG-NI- FY THE LORD

<u>MS</u>: Holograph in collection of PP.
<u>Parts</u>: SATB, rehearsal part for organ.
<u>Pub</u>: New York: G. Schirmer, 1887.
<u>Parts</u>: SATB and organ.
<u>Ded</u>: to Reverend M. Riley.
<u>Copy inf</u>: Copyright renewed 1915.
<u>Copy</u>: NN.

124. "Merry Christmas"

<u>Pub</u>: Boston: Silver Burdett and Co., 1911.
<u>Parts</u>: Choir, eight voice parts.
<u>Text</u>: Margaret E. Sangster.

125. "New Church"

How Glor-ious on the Moun-tains

Pub: Hosanna for Children. New York: New Church Publication Society,
1905.
Copy: CNJ.

126. "Ninetieth Psalm, The"

MS: MS orchestra parts by copyist in collection of FLP. Violin I, 8 parts;
violin II, 7 parts; viola, 6 parts; violoncello, 5 parts; bass, 4 parts; 1
part each: flute I, II; oboe I, II; clarinet I, II; bassoon I, II; contrabas-
soon; horn I, II, III, IV; trumpet I, II; trombone I, II, III, IV; tuba;
tympani.
Parts: SATB with organ or piano.
Pub: Philadelphia: W.W. Gilchrist, 1915.
Ded: Mendelssohn Club of Philadelphia.
Misc: ARG listing notations: "presented by Mendelssohn Club, Father too
sick to go"; "plates destroyed 1931."
Perf: MC, April 14, 1915.
Copy: LC.

127. "No! No! It is Not Dying"

Pub: New York: Charles S. Elliot and Co., 1897.
Parts: SATB.
Text: H.A.C. Malan.

128. "No! Not Despairingly"

No! Not De-spair-ing-ly

Pub: Boston: Oliver Ditson, 1896.
Parts: SATB with organ.
Text: Horatius Bonar.
Price: $.12.
Copy: DLC.

129. "Now Rest Ye Pilgrim Host"[3]

Pub: New Hosanna. New York: New Church Board of Publication, 1902.
Text: R.W. Raymond.
Ocas. perf: Anniversary.
Copy: PBa.

130. "Now To Heaven Our Prayer Ascending"

Pub: New Hosanna. New York: New Church Board of Publication, 1902.
Text: W.E. Hickson.
Copy: PBa.

131. "Nunc Dimittis (F major)"

Misc: Title listed on "Sweet Saviour, Bless Us Ere We Go," published by
G. Schirmer, New York.

132. "O Jesu, Thou Art Standing"

Pub: New York: G. Schirmer, 1909.
Parts: SATB and alto solo with organ.
Text: H.H. How.
Copy inf: Copyright renewed 1936.
Price: $.15.
Royalty rate: 10 percent.
Royalties: February 1913, $3.54; 1914, .48; 1915, 6.81; 1916, 3.05; February 1922, 1.95; February 1923, 2.43; February 1924, 1.50; February 1925, 4.80; February 1926, 6.90; February 1927, 50 copies sold for 7.50; February 1928, 150 copies sold for 22.50; 1929, 49 copies sold for 7.35; February 1930, 49 copies sold for 7.35.
Copy: DLC.

133. "O Bread to Pilgrims Given"

---

[3]Published as "Pilgrim Host," in Presbyterian Hymnal. See p. 111.

Pub: New Hosanna. New York: New Church Board of Publication, 1902.
Text: Josiah Conder.
Copy: PBa.

134. "O Christmas-Tide!"

O   CHRIST- MAS TIDE O   CHRIST- MAS TIDE

Pub: New Hosanna. New York: New Church Board of Publication, 1902.
Text: W.W. Gilchrist.
Copy: PBa.

135. "O Little Town of Bethlehem!"

O   LIT- TLE TOWN OF   BETH- LE- HEM

Pub: New Hosanna. New York: New Church Board of Publication, 1902.
Text: Bishop Phillips Brooks.
Copy: PBa.

136. "O Lord the Proud are Risen"

O   LORD   THE PROUD ARE RISEN

MS: MS by copyist, Thomas A'Becket, in collection of PP.
Parts: SATB and organ.
Text: from Psalm 86:14-16.
Misc: Notes on MS, "$30," "original in possession of D.D. Wood, Phila."

137. "O Many and Many a Year Ago"

Misc: ARG listing, Christmas.

138. "O Saviour! Precious Saviour!"

O SAV- IOUR   PRE- CIOUS SAV- IOUR

MS: Holograph in collection of PP.
Parts: SATB and soprano solo with organ.
Text: Francis R. Havergal.

139. "O That My Head Were Waters"

Pub: New York: H.W. Gray, 1909.
Parts: SATB and organ.
Ocas. perf: Lenten anthem.
Copy inf: Copyright renewed 1922.
Misc: from "The Lamb of God."

140. "Pilgrim Host"[4]

Now REST YE PIL- GRIM HOST

Pub: Presbyterian Hymnal. Philadelphia: Presbyterian Board of Public
and Sabbath School Work, 1895.
Text: Rossiter W. Raymond.
Copy: DLC.

141. "Ponder My Words"

PON - DER MY WORDS   PON - DER MY WORDS O LORD

Pub: New York: G. Schirmer, 1915.
Parts: SATB and soprano solo with organ.
Text: Psalm 5:1-3.
Copy inf: Copyright renewed 1943.
Perf: CNJ, January 11, 1946.
Copy: DLC.

142. "Prayer and Praise"

GIVE EAR O SHEP-HERD OF IS-RA-EL

MS: Holograph in collection of DLC, dated "Germantown, November 3,
1889."
Parts: Chorus and solo voices.
Pub: New York: G. Schirmer, 1888.
Parts: SATB and solo voices with piano or organ.
Ded: to the Germantown Choral.
Misc: ARG listing, orchestra parts in MS.
Copy: DLC.

---

[4]Published as "Now Rest Ye Pilgrim Host," in New Hosanna. See p. 109.

143. "Recessional"

Pub: New York: G. Schirmer, 1902.
Parts: SATB with piano.
Text: Rudyard Kipling.
Copy inf: Copyright renewed 1929.
Misc: Song setting, same melody.
Copy: DLC.

144. "Rolling On"

Misc: ARG listing, published by Arthur P. Schmidt, New York, 1899.

145. "Saint Clements"

Pub: Book of Common Praise. Reformed Episcopal Publication Society,
1885.
Text: Isaac Watts.
Copy: PP.

146. "Saint Louis Christmas"

Pub: Book of Worship. New York: New Church Board of Publication,
1950.
Text: Phillips Brooks.
Copy: CNJ.

147. "Sanctus"

Pub: Magnificat. New York: New Church Board of Publication, 1910.
Copy: CNJ.

148.   "Saviour, Again to Thy Dear Name"

Pub: New York: G. Schirmer, 1889.
Copy inf: Copyright renewed 1917 by Anna R. Gilchrist.

149.   "Saviour Like a Shepherd Lead Us"

Perf: MMS, April 30, 1902.

150.   "Saviour Whom I Fain Would Love"

MS: Holograph in collection of PP.
Parts: SATB chorus or quartet and soprano solo with organ.
Text: Toplady.

151.   "Sewell"

Pub: Magnificat.   New York: New Church Board of Publication, 1910.
Copy: CNJ.
Pub: Book of Worship.   New York: New Church Board of Publication,
1950.
Text: F. Sewell.
Copy: CNJ.

152.   "Shadows of the Evening Hours"

Pub: Boston: Oliver Ditson, 1905.
Parts: SATB and alto solo with organ.
Text: Adelaide A. Procter.
Price: $.12.
Copy: DLC.

153. "Sheepfold"

SAV - IOUR   LIKE   A   SHEP - HERD   LEAD US

Pub: Magnificat. New York: New Church Board of Publication, 1910.
Text: D.A. Thrupp.
Copy: CNJ.

154. "Shout the Glad Tidings"

Pub: New York: G. Schirmer, 1887.
Parts: SATB.
Text: W.A. Muhlenburg.
Ocas. perf: Christmas.

155. "Sing, O Daughter of Zion"

Misc: ARG listing, 1877.

156. "Sing, O Sing, this Blessed Morn"

Pub: New York: G. Schirmer, 1905.
Parts: SATB and soprano solo with organ.
Ocas. perf: Christmas.
Copy inf: Copyright renewed 1933 by Anna R. Gilchrist.
Price: $.25.
Royalty rate: 10 percent.
Royalties: February 1913, $.11; 1914, .08; 1915, 1.98; 1916, .94; 1917,
.96; 1918, .90; 1919, 1.13; February 1921, .38; February 1925, .25; Feb-
ruary 1926, 2.4850; February 1928, 50 copies sold for 12.50; February
1930, 50 copies sold for 12.50; February 1931, 7.20.

157. "Sing We Alleluia"

ALLEGRO
         BASS

To HIM WHO FOR OUR SINS WAS SLAIN TO HIM FOR ALL HIS DY-ING PAIN

Pub: New York: G. Schirmer, 1883.
Parts: SATB and organ.
Ocas. perf: Easter.
Copy inf: Copyright renewed 1911.
Price: $.12.
Royalty rate: 10 percent.
Royalties: February 1927, 50 copies sold for $7.50.
Copy: DLC.

158. "Sinners Turn, Why Will Ye Die?"

Pub: New York: G. Schirmer, 1905.
Parts: SATB and mezzo-soprano solo with organ.
Text: Wesley.
Price: $.15.
Royalty rate: 10 percent.
Royalties: 1919, $.60.
Copy: DLC.

159. "Smyth"

Pub: Magnificat. New York: New Church Board of Publication, 1910.
Text: F.S. Pierpont.
Copy: CNJ.

160. "Softly the Echoes Come"

Misc: ARG listing.
Ocas. perf: Christmas.

161. "Sunset"

Pub: Magnificat. New York: New Church Board of Publication, 1910.
Text: Isaac Watts.
Copy: CNJ.

162. "Supplication"

Pub: Magnificat. New York: New Church Board of Publication, 1910.
Book of Worship. New York: New Church Board of Publication, 1950.
Hosanna. Boston: The Swedenborg Press, 1968.
Text: L.M. Willis.
Copy: CNJ (all books).

163. "Sweet Saviour, Bless Us Ere We Go"

Pub: New York: G. Schirmer, 1887.
Parts: SATB with organ.
Text: Frederick W. Faber.
Copy inf: Copyright renewed 1915.
Copy: DLC, NN.

164. "Te Deum (A major)"

Misc: ARG listing, Festival.

165. "Te Deum (A♭ major)"

Misc: Title listed on "Sweet Saviour, Bless Us Ere We Go," published by
G. Schirmer, New York.

166. "Te Deum (B♭ major)"

Misc: ARG listing, 1886.
Price: $.60.

167. "Te Deum (C major)"

Pub: Philadelphia: William Wallace Gilchrist, 1886.
Copy inf: Copyright renewed 1914.

168. "Te Deum (F major, Number one)."

Pub: Philadelphia: William Wallace Gilchrist, 1883.
Copy inf: Copyright renewed 1911.
Price: $.20.
Royalty rate: 10 percent.

169. "Te Deum (F major, Number two)"

Misc: Title listed on "Magnificat in G major," published by G. Schirmer,
New York.
Price: $.25.
Royalty rate: 10 percent.

170. "Te Deum (G major, Number one)"

Misc: ARG listing.
Price: $.25.
Royalty rate: 10 percent.

171. "Te Deum (G major, Number two)"

Pub: Philadelphia: William Wallace Gilchrist, 1883.
Copy inf: Copyright renewed 1911.

172. "Te Deum Laudamus (F major)"

Misc: ARG listing, 1898.
Price: $.12.

173. "Te Dominum (C major)"

Pub: Magnificat. New York: New Church Board of Publication, 1910.
Book of Worship. New York: The Swedenborg Press, 1968.
Copy: CNJ (both books).

174. "Te Dominum (F major)"

Pub: New York: G. Schirmer, 1882.
Parts: SATB with organ.
Ded: First New Jerusalem Society, Philadelphia.
Perf: MMS, June 7, 1905.
Copy: CNJ.

175. "Thanksgiving II"

Pub: Magnificat. New York: New Church Board of Publication, 1910.
Copy: CNJ.

176. "Thanksgiving III"

Pub: Magnificat. New York: New Church Board of Publication, 1910.
Copy: CNJ.

177. "There's a Song in the Air"

Pub: New Hosanna. New York: New Church Board of Publication, 1902.
Text: Dr. J.G. Holland.
Copy: PBa.

178. "To Jesus Christ the Lord"

Pub: Magnificat. New York: New Church Board of Publication, 1910.
Copy: CNJ.

179. "Uplifted Gates, The"

Pub: New York: G. Schirmer, 1884.
Parts: SATB with four hand accompaniment.
Perf: MC, March 28, 1883; MC, May 1, 1883; Grand Testimonial Concert,
January 15, 1886; Testimonial Concert, May 21, 1914.
Copy: DLC.

180. "Upsal"

Pub: Magnificat. New York: New Church Board of Publication, 1910.
Text: Heber-Whately.
Copy: CNJ.

181. "Vision, Number 2"

Pub: Magnificat. New York: New Church Board of Publication, 1910.
Text: Edmund H. Sears.
Copy: CNJ.

182. "Wakefield"

Pub: Presbyterian Hymnal. Philadelphia: Presbyterian Board of Public
and Sabbath School Work, 1895.
Text: H.A. Cesar Malan.
Copy: DLC.

183. "Way of Peace"

Pub: Presbyterian Hymnal. Philadelphia: Presbyterian Board of Public
and Sabbath School Work, 1895.
Text: John Julian.

184. "Weary of Earth"

Pub: Boston: Oliver Ditson, 1898.
Parts: SATB and soprano solo with organ.
Text: S.J. Stone.
Price: $.12.
Copy: DLC.

185. "What e'er my God Ordains is Right"

Pub: New York: H.W. Gray and Co., 1914.
Parts: SATB or quartet and contralto solo with keyboard.
Text: S. Rodigast, translated by C. Winkworth.
Copy: DLC.

186. "When the Weary Seeking Rest"

Pub: Philadelphia: Geibel and Lehman, 1904.
Parts: SATB with keyboard.
Text: Horatius Bonar.
Copy: DLC.

187. "Where Bloom Celestial Roses"

Pub: Hosanna for Children. New York: New Church Board of Publication,
1905.
Copy: CNJ.

188. "Whitsuntide" [5]

Pub: Magnificat. New York: New Church Board of Publication, 1910.
Text: J.H. Hopkins, Jr.
Copy: CNJ.

189. "Worcester"

Pub: Magnificat. New York: New Church Board of Publication, 1910.
Text: W.L. Worcester.
Copy: CNJ.

190. "Ye Mountains Falls on Us"

Misc: ARG listing.

[5]Published as "Hopkins," in Book of Common Praise. See p. 101.

VOCAL: CHORAL MUSIC (SECULAR)

191.   "Ah! Twinkling Star"

Parts: SATB.
Perf: Oratorio Society, First Presbyterian Church, February 16, 1903.

192.   "Approach of Spring"

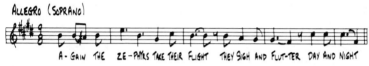

Pub: New York: G. Schirmer, 1894.
Parts: Women, four parts with piano for rehearsal only.
Copy inf: Copyright renewed 1922 by Anna R. Gilchrist.
Price: $.15 per copy.
Royalties: February 1926, $.5250; February 1928, 45 copies sold, royalty 6.75; February 1931, 104.70; royalty 10 percent.
Copy: NN.

193.   "Bells, The"

Pub: New York: G. Schirmer, 1913.
Parts: Women, four parts with piano.
Text: Edgar A. Poe.
Copy inf: Copyright renewed 1941.
Perf: MMS, February 28, 1917.

194.   "Bugle Song"

MS: Holograph in collection of PP.
Pub: New York: G. Schirmer, 1886.
Parts: Men, four parts.
Text: Tennyson.
Misc: Note on MS, $15.
Copy: DLC.

195. "Charm Me Asleep"

Pub: Boston: Oliver Ditson, 1913.
Parts: Women, three parts.
Text: Robert Herrick.
Agree: Sell and assign agreement January 25, 1913, $50 for "Charm Me
Asleep," and "Cherry Ripe." (Presser Documents.)
Price: $.12.
Royalty rate: 10 percent.
Perf: MC, May 1, 1913; MMS, November 29, 1916, January 11, 1921.

196. "Cherry Ripe"

Pub: Boston: Oliver Ditson, 1913.
Parts: Women, three parts.
Text: Robert Herrick.
Agree: Sell and assign agreement January 25, 1913, $50 for "Cherry Ripe"
and "Charm Me Asleep." (Ibid.)
Perf: MC, May 1, 1913; Matinee Musicale Club, March 31, 1914; MC, May
18, 1946.

197. "Come O'er the Sea"

Pub: New York: G. Schirmer, 1886.
Copy inf: Copyright renewed 1914.
Misc: ARG listing, baritone solo and chorus.

198. "Come Shout Come Sing of the Great Sea King (Song with an accom-
      paniment for four hands)"

MS: Holographs in collection of PP.
Parts: Men, four parts with piano, four hands; FLP has 2 piano parts, 1
first tenor part, 3 second tenor parts, 2 first bass parts, 1 second bass
part.
Text: Barry Cornwall.

199. "Death of the Rose, The"

Pub: Boston: Oliver Ditson, 1913.
Parts: Women, four parts.
Text: Robert Herrick.
Agree: Agreement February 13, 1913 for 10 percent royalty after first 500
copies sold. (Presser Documents.)
Price: $.12.
Royalty rate: 10 percent.
Royalties: January 1904, $.64; January 1917, .24; July 1917, .36; 1927
sold 100 copies, 1.20; July 1929, .60; July 1913, .24.

200. "Dreaming, Forever Vainly Dreaming"

DREAM - ING FOR - EV- ER VAIN-LY DREAM -   ING

Pub: New York: G. Schirmer, 1885.
Parts: Men, four parts with piano for rehearsal only.
Text: Barry Cornwall.
Misc: Won prize from Mendelssohn Club of New York in 1880. [6]
Copy: DLC.

201. "Drinking Song"

FILL THE BUM-PER FAIR   EV — RY DROP WE SPRIN-KLE

Pub: New York: G. Schirmer, 1886.
Parts: Men, four parts.
Text: Thomas Moore.
Copy: DLC.

202. "Fountain, The"

Pub: Philadelphia: Theodore Presser, 1899.
Text: James Russell Lowell.
Misc: Listed in Catalog of Copyright Entries as chorus for women's
voices with piano.
Agree: Statement, April 18, 1899: paper and printing for 500 copies at
cost of $7.40, they kept 148 at $.05 to cover cost; statement, January 27,
1902: 300 copies printed at cost of $6.70, they kept 134 to cover cost.
(Presser Documents.)

203. "Future, The"

SAIL FAST, SAIL FAST, SAIL   FAST — , SAIL FAST!

Pub: New York: H.W. Gray Co., 1908.
Parts: SATB with piano.
Text: Sidney Lanier.
Copy: NN.

---

[6]William F. Collins, Laurel Winners (Cincinnati: John Church Co., 1900),
p. 84.

204. "Home They Brought Her Warrior Dead"

MS: Holograph in collection of PP.
Parts: Soprano and tenor with piano.
Text: Tennyson.
Misc: Grouped with "Shine, Shine."

205. "Hunting Song"

Pub: New York: G. Schirmer, 1910.
Text: Barry Cornwall.
Copy inf: Copyright renewed 1938.

206. "In Autumn"

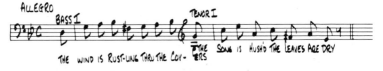

Pub: New York: G. Schirmer, 1885.
Parts: Men, four parts.
Misc: Won prize from Mendelssohn Club of New York in 1880. (Collins, Laurel Winners, p. 84.)
Copy: DLC.

207. "In the Blush of Evening"

Pub: Boston: Oliver Ditson, 1897.
Parts: Women, four parts with soprano solo.
Text: Johann W. von Goethe.
Price: $.12.
Royalty rate: 10 percent.
Royalties: 1897, $12, 10 percent of each sale; January 1915, .36; January 1917, .24; July 1917, .06; July 1920, .18; 1927, .36; July 1931, .80.
Perf: MC, January 17, 1907.

208. "Journey of Life, The"

Pub: New York: G. Schirmer, 1886.
Parts: Men, four parts.
Text: William Cullen Bryant.
Copy inf: Copyright renewed 1914.
Copy: LC.

209. "Knight of Toggenburg, The"

MS: Holographs in collection of PP.
Parts: Women, four parts and alto solo with orchestra (flute; oboe; clari-
net; bassoon; horn I, II; violin I, II; viola; violoncello; bass; pianoforte).
Autograph parts: violin I, 4 parts; violin II, 4 parts; viola, 2 parts;
violoncello, 2 parts; bass, 2 parts; flute; oboe; clarinet; bassoon; horn I,
horn II; tympani D^b; tympani C.
Pub: Boston: Oliver Ditson Co., 1911.
Parts: Women, four parts and alto solo with piano.
Text: From the German of Friedrich von Schiller.
Misc: ARG listing, date 1878 MS book.
Price: $.50.
Royalty rate: $.05.
Royalties: January 1914, $6.00; January 1917, 4.50; January 1918, 2.50;
July 1918, .10; January 1919, .10; 1927, .10; July 1931, .24; July 1932,
.06.
Perf: MMS, April 20, 1898.
Copy: Piano-vocal score DLC, MB, PP, RPB.

210. "Legend of the Bended Bow"

Pub: New York: G. Schirmer, 1888.
Parts: Men, four parts and soprano solo with piano, four hands.
Text: Mrs. Hemans.
Copy inf: Copyright renewed 1916.
Perf: Pennsylvania State Music Teachers Association Annual Convention
and Music Festival, December 29, 1893.
Copy: DLC, MB.

211. "Lullaby"

Copy inf: Copyright renewed 1922.
Misc: Title listed on "Approach of Spring" published by G. Schirmer,
New York. ARG listing, women, four parts.
Agree: Agreement June 23, 1911: Gilchrist gave plates to Presser as
custodian to produce copies as demand required at royalty rate of 15 per-
cent. (Presser Documents.)
Royalties: 1931, forty copies sold, $.60.

212. "Miranda"

Pub: New York: H.W. Gray Co., 1908.
Parts: SATB.
Text: Sidney Lanier.
Perf: MMS, January 20, 1909.

213. "Morning Song"

Pub: New York: G. Schirmer, 1894.
Parts: Women, four parts.
Copy inf: Copyright renewed 1922 by Anna R. Gilchrist.
Royalties: February 1925, $1.20; February 1926, 1.50; February 1927, 50
copies sold, 7.50; February 1923, 98 copies sold, 14.70.
Perf: MMS, May 13, 1897.

214. "National Hymn"

Pub: Philadelphia: W.H. Boner, 1887. Included in History of the Celebration of the Promulgation of the Constitution by Carson, Hampton, Lawrence in John Hay Library, Brown University.
Parts: Men, four parts.
Text: F. Marion Crawford.
Misc: Setting for new national hymn written for Memorial Day Ceremonies
in Independence Square, Philadelphia, September 17, 1887. Verses spoken
to music, chorus sung.
Copy: RPB.

215. "Nights, The"

Pub: Boston: Oliver Ditson, 1897.
Parts: Women, three parts.
Text: Barry Cornwall.
Misc: Plates melted 1922. (ARG ledger.)
Price: $.12.
Royalty rate: 10 percent.
Royalties: January 1914, $.54; January 1915, 3.96; July 1915, .18; Janu-
ary 1917, .24; July 1917, .18; January 1918, .66; January 1919, .42; July
1920, .30; January 1921, .18; July 1921, .24.

216.   "O Captain! My Captain!"

MS: Autograph in colleciton of PP.
Parts: SATB with piano.
Text: [Walt Whitman.]

217.   "Ode to the Sun, An"

Pub: New York: G. Schirmer, 1885.
Parts: Men, four parts with piano, four hands.
Text: Mrs. Hemans.
Misc: Won prize from Mendelssohn Club of New York in 1880. (Collins,
Laurel Winners, p. 84.)

218.   "Pyramus and Thisby"

Misc: ARG listing, comic-tragedy in two acts.

219.   "Rolling On"

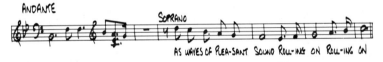

Pub: Boston: Arthur P. Schmidt, 1899.
Parts: Women, four parts with piano.
Text: Charles F. Cox.
Copy: NN.

220.   "Rose, The"

MS: Holograph in collection of PP.
Parts: SATB and mezzo-soprano solo with orchestra (flute; oboe; clarinet;
bassoon; horn I, II, III, IV; violin I, II; viola; violoncello; bass).
Pub: New York: G. Schirmer, 1887.
Parts: SATB and mezzo-soprano solo with organ.
Text: J.R. Lowell.
Ded: Miss Sarah R. Yarnall, Philadelphia.
Copy inf: Copyright renewed 1915.
Perf: Tuesday Club, June 4, 1889; MMS and MC joint concert, May 7,
1914; Testimonial Concert to William Wallace Gilchrist, May 21, 1914; Ora-
torio Society of Philadelphia, February 16, 1903.
Copy: ICN, MH, NN.

221. "Rose To A Rose, A"

Pub: New York: H.W. Gray, 1908.
Parts: SATB.
Text: Sidney Lanier.
Perf: MMS, January 20, 1909; MC, May 1, 1919.

222. "Sea Fairies"

Parts: Women, four parts with piano, four hands.
Text: Tennyson.
Misc: ARG listing, G. Schirmer, New York 1879-80.
Price: $.20.
Royalty rate: 10 percent.
Royalties: February 1922, $14.14; February 1924, 2.90; February 1925, 1.10; February 1926, 1.08; February 1930, 4.60; February 1931, 12.00.
Perf: MC, December 11, 1879, May 5, 1886; MMS, May 22, 1895.

223. "Shine! Shine!"

MS: Holograph in collection of PP.
Parts: Soprano and baritone; soprano and tenor.
Misc: Grouped with "Home they brought her warrior dead."

224. "Sit Down, Sad Soul"

Pub: Boston: Oliver Ditson, 1897.
Parts: Women, three parts.
Text: Barry Cornwall.
Price: $.12.
Royalty rate: 10 percent.
Royalties: January 1917, $.30.

225. "Sleep and Poetry"

MS: Autograph in collection of PP.
Parts: Women, three parts.
Text: John Keats.

226. "Spring Song"

Pub: New York: G. Schirmer, 1881.
Parts: Trio for mezzo-soprano or alto, tenor and baritone.

Perf: Grand Testimonial Concert in honor of William Wallace Gilchrist at
Musical Fund Hall, January 15, 1886; Musicale, Second Reformed Church of
Philadelphia, February 18, 1886; Concert in Wayne, Delaware County, Ap-
ril 27, 1886; Concert for Saint Luke's Hospital, Jacksonville, Florida, 1886;
Alpha Boat Club Concert, January 25, 1887; Madrigal and Ballad Concert,
June 2, 1887; Musicale, Conservatory Hall, February 15, 1889; Madrigal
Concert for Philadelphia Cricket Club, 1899; MMS, November 18, 1896.

227. "Spring Song"

Pub: New York: G. Schirmer, 1886.
Parts: Men, four parts.
Copy inf: Copyright renewed 1914.

228. "Summer's Morn, A"

Misc: Listed in ARG ledger.
Price: $.12.
Royalty rate: 10 percent.
Royalties: July 1917, $1.07; January 1918, .12; January 1919, 2.04; 1927,
35 copies sold, .42; July 1929, .96; July 1931, .42; July 1932, .11; July
1933, 1.22.

229. "Syrens, The"

Pub: New York: G. Schirmer, 1904.
Parts: Women, four parts with ensemble (flute, horn, violin, violoncello,
and piano).
Text: J. Russell Lowell.
Ded: Ladies of the Mendelssohn Club.
Copy inf: Copyright renewed 1932 by Anna R. Gilchrist.
Perf: Matinee Musical Club, March 31, 1914.
Copy: DLC; MH.

230. Three Summer Songs ("A Summer's Morn, A Summer's Day, A Sum-
      mer's Night")

Pub: Boston: Oliver Ditson, 1914.
Parts: Women, three parts.
Text: Walt Whitman and Celia Thaxter.
Copy inf: Copyright renewed 1941 by Susan B. Gilchrist.
Agree: Agreement of sale September 9, 1913, 10 percent royalty. (Presser
Documents.)
Price: $.20.
Royalty rate: 10 percent.
Royalties: January 1914, $3.20; July 1915, 5.10; January 1917, .30; July
1917, 1.60; 1924, .60; July 1927, 1.10; July 1931, 1.80.

231. "To Song"

Pub: Printed privately.
Parts: SATB with piano.
Text: William Wallace Gilchrist.
Misc: ARG listing, orchestra parts.
Perf: MC, April 8, 1907; April 14, 1915; February 9, 1936; Anna R. Gilchrist wrote, "This song is used as the opening number at all our concerts," in 1936. (The Helper 97, no. 9 [1936]: 2.)
Copy: Given to author by Mendelssohn Club.

232. "What is More Gentle"

MS: Autograph, incomplete, in collection of PP.
Parts: One page for piano, soprano I, soprano II and alto.
Pub: Boston: Oliver Ditson, 1906.
Parts: SATB with piano.
Text: John Keats.
Price: $.12.
Royalty rate: 10 percent.
Perf: MC, December 9, 1915.
Copy: DLC.

233. "Separation and Reunion (Scena for Soprano and Orchestra)"

MS: Holograph in collection of PP dated 1885.
Parts: Soprano and piano score; soprano and orchestra score and orchestra parts (violin I, 3 parts; violin II, 3 parts; viola, 2 parts; violoncello, 2 parts; 1 part each: bass (or violoncello); oboe; clarinet I, II; bassoon; horn I, II; tympani.
Text: William Wallace Gilchrist.
Misc: Note on score, "Orchestra parts may be had after publication."
Performed Grand Testimonial Concert for William Wallace Gilchrist, January 15, 1886.

VOCAL: SONGS (VOICE AND KEYBOARD)

234. "All for thee"

IF LIFE FOR ME BOTH JOY OR LIGHT

MS: Autograph in collection of PP.
Misc: ARG listing, 1877 MS book.

235. "All My Heart This Day Rejoices"

ALL MY HEART THIS DAY RE - JOI - CES

Pub: Cincinnati: John Church Co., 1898.
Text: Gerhardt-Winkworth.
Agree: Assigned to John Church April 20, 1898 for $40 with three other
songs. (Presser Documents. Other works were "Bethlehem," "From Heaven
Above," "Once in Royal David's City.")
Misc: Published as Three Carols for Christmas with "From Heaven Above"
and "Once in Royal David's City."
Copy: DLC, NN.

236. "All Service Ranks the Same with God"

ALL SER - VICE RANKS THE SAME WITH GOD

MS: Holograph in collection of PP.
Parts: Solo and reader with organ.
Text: From Robert Browning's Pippa Passes.
Misc: Note on MS "A copy of this sent to Baylor University, Waco, Texas,
to be included in the music section of the Browning Library--May 1933."
ARG listing date, 1877.
Copy: MB.

237. "Allegheny"

Misc: Entered in the Catalog of Copyright Entries, August 31, 1901.

238. "Angels From the Realms of Glory"

AN - GELS FROM THE REALMS OF GLO-RY   WING YOU FLIGHT OER   ALL THE EARTH

Pub: New York: G. Schirmer, 1883.
Text: James Montgomery.
Misc: Published as Three Christmas Carols and One Hymn.
Copy: DLC, NN.

239. "Another Morning Hymn"

MODERATELY SLOW

DEAR   FA - THER   AL - WAYS   NEAR   US

Pub: Songs for the Children.   Philadelphia: Theodore Presser, 1897.
Text: Sophia Bixby.
Copy: Griffin collection.

240. "April"

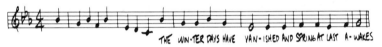

THE WIN-TER DAYS HAVE VAN-ISHED AND SPRING AT LAST A-WAKES

Pub: Educational Music Course.   Boston: Ginn and Co., 1904.
Text: Julius Altman.
Copy: DLC.

241. "Autumn Song"

ALLEGRETTO

A LIT-TLE BIRD FLEW OER THE LEA —

Pub: Boston: Arthur P. Schmidt, 1885.
Text: from German of Tieck.
Perf: MMS November 15, 1899.
Copy: DLC, NN.

242. "Barcarolle"

COME OER THE SEA

MS: Holograph in collection of PP.
Parts: Soprano and piano.
Text: Tennyson.

243. "Bird's Nest, The"

HERE'S A PRE-TTY CRA-DLE NEST SNUG AND WARM AND ROUND

Pub: Songs for the Children. Philadelphia: Theodore Presser, 1897.
Text: Emily Huntington Miller.
Copy. Griffin collection.

244. "Blessed Morning"

MODERATO

BLESS-ED MORN-ING BLESS-ED MORN-ING WHEN THE SAV-IOUR MEEK AND MILD

Pub: New York: G. Schirmer, 1883.
Copy: DLC, NN.

245. "Blue-eyed Lassie, The"

ALLEGRETTO

I GAED A WAE-FUL GATE YES-TREEN

Pub: New York: G. Schirmer, 1895.
Text: Robert Burns.
Copy inf: Copyright renewed 1923 by ARG.
Misc: Published as Three Scotch Songs with "Dainty Davie" and "My Heart
is Sair."
Perf: Musical, Philadelphia Composers, January 29, 1898; Matinee Musicale,
March 31, 1914; MMS and MC joint concert, May 7, 1914.
Copy: DLC, NN.

246. "Bonnie Boatie, The"

ALLEGRETTO

O THE BON-NIE SAIL-OR BOY

MS: Holograph in collection of PP.
Misc: Three versions. Note on cover, "Song is excellent but too advanced
for little people in the Primary School. Simpler song required"; note on
page one, "Rote song value doubtful." Second version, last eight measures simplified and altered; third version beginning altered and last eight
measures as original.

247. "Brightest and Best"

BRIGHT-EST AND BEST OF THE SONS OF THE MORN-ING

Pub: New York: G. Schirmer, 1883.
Text: [Bishop Heber.]
Copy: DLC, NN.

248. "Brightest and Best of the Sons of the Morning"

BRIGHT-EST AND BEST OF THE SONS OF THE   MORN - ING.

Pub: New Hosanna. New York: New Church Board of Publication, 1902.
Text: Bishop Heber.
Ocas. perf: Christmas.
Copy: PBa.

249. "Broken Doll"

MY DOL-LY BROKE HER HEAD TO-DAY

Pub: Philadelphia: Theodore Presser, 1899.
Text: William Wallace Gilchrist.
Copy inf: Copyright renewed 1927 by Susan B. Gilchrist.
Agree: Added to Songs for the Children, March 1899. (Presser Documents.)
Price: $.20.
Royalty rate: .03 percent.
Royalties: September 1914, $.18; September 1915, .48; September 1917,
.33; September 1918, .24; September 1919, .42; 1920, .66; September 1921,
.48; September 1922, .36; September 1923, .45; 1927, .48; September 1930,
1.36; September 1931, 1.21; September 1932, 1.05; 1935, 1.05; September
1936, 1.57; 1937, 1.05.
Copy: PP.

250. "Bugle Song"

THE   SPLEN-DOR FALLS ON CAS-TLE WALLS

Pub: New York: G. Schirmer, 1884.
Parts: Soprano or tenor in G, baritone or alto in F.
Text: Tennyson.
Perf: As "Blow, Bugle, Blow," MC, April 28, 1910.
Copy: DLC, NN, PP (all in G).

251. "Canst Thou Leave Me Thus, My Katy"

Pub: Philadelphia: Theodore Presser, 1898.
Text: Robert Burns.
Copy inf: Copyright renewed 1926 by Susan B. Gilchrist.
Agree: Agreement for Six Scotch Songs, words by Robert Burns, October
29, 1897, no royalty on first 100 copies, 10 percent thereafter. (Presser
Documents.)
Perf: MMS, January 22, 1908.
Copy: DLC.

252. "Carol Forth the Strain"

Misc: Title listed on "Raise we now our Hearts and Voices," published by
William A. Pond, New York.

253. "Carpenter, The"

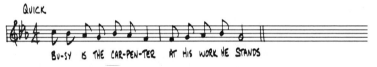

Pub: Songs for the Children. Philadelphia: Theodore Presser, 1897.
Text: Emilie Poulsson.
Copy: Griffin collection.

254. "Child and Mother"

Pub: Songs of Childhood. Edited by Reginald DeKoven. New York:
Charles Scribner's Sons, 1896.
Text: Eugene Field.
Copy: DLC.

255. "Children Can You Truly Tell"

Pub: Hosanna for Children. New York: New Church Board of Publica-
tion, 1905. Hosanna. New York: New Church Press, 1920.
Misc: Entered in Catalog of Copyright Entries, November 22, 1875.
Copy: CNJ (both books).

256. "'Christ is Born,' The Angels Say"

CHRIST IS BORN THE AN- GELS SAY

Pub: Six Christmas Carols by Gilchrist, Shelley and Staton. Boston:
Oliver Ditson, 1908.
Copy: NN.

257. "Christ the Sun of Righteousness"

O THE BEAU-TY AND THE GLO-RY

MS: Autograph in collection of PP.
Parts: Soprano and organ.

258. "Christmas Morning"

TWAS ON   A CHRIST-MAS MORN - ING

Pub: London: Weekes and Co., 1908.
Text: A.E. Stilwell.
Copy: DLC.

259. "Christmas Song"

Misc: Entered in the Copyright Catalog, November 28, 1903.

260. "Come See the Place Where Jesus Lay"

COME SEE THE PLACE WHERE JE-SUS LAY AND HEAR TH'AN-GEL-IC WA-TCHERS SAY

Pub: New York: G. Schirmer, 1887.
Text: Richard Crashaw.
Copy: DLC.

261. "Consolation"

FALSE FLEET-ING YOUTH AH! WHITH-ER FLED

MS: Holograph in collection of PP.
Parts: Soprano and piano.
Text: Bayard Taylor.

262. "Constancy"

LOVE THEE DEAR-EST LOVE THEE

Pub: New York: Edward Schubert, 1886.
Copy inf: Copyright renewed, 1914.
Copy: LC.

263. "Cottager's Lullaby"

THE DAYS ARE COLD   THE NIGHTS ARE LONG

MS: Holograph in collection of PP.
Parts: Soprano and piano.
Text: Dorothy Wordsworth.
Perf: MMS, January 22, 1908.

264. "Dainty Davie"

NOW ROSY MAY COMES IN wi' FLOWRS TO DECK HER GAY GREEN SPREADING BOW

Pub: New York: G. Schirmer, 1895.
Parts: Soprano or baritone.
Text: Robert Burns.
Copy inf: Copyright renewed 1933 by ARG.
Misc: Published as Three Scotch Songs, with "The Blue-eyed Lassie," and
"My Heart's Sair."
Perf: Musical, Philadelphia Composers, January 29, 1898; Matinee Musicale,
February 3, 1925.
Copy: DLC; OrU.

265. "Daisy, The"

IN SHOALS AND BANDS A NO-VICE TRAIN

MS: Holograph in collection of PP.
Parts: Soprano and piano.
Text: N.M.

266. "Dawn is Breaking O'er Us, The"

Misc: ARG listing.

267. "Day of Resurrection"

THE   DAY OF RE-SUR- REC- TION

Pub: Philadelphia: William H. Boner, 1878. Hosanna. New York: New
Church Board of Publication, 1920.
Text: Saint John Damascene.
Ocas. perf: Easter song.
Copy: CNJ (Hosanna), DLC (Boner edition).

268. "Daybreak"

A WIND CAME UP OUT OF THE   SEA

Pub: Fifth Music Reader. Boston: Ginn and Co., 1906.
Text: Longfellow.
Copy: LC.

269. "Dear Long Ago, The"

IN THE GRAY OF THE GLOOM-ING OER LOW LANDS AND HIGH LAND

Pub: Boston, Arthur P. Schmidt, 1885.
Text: Mrs. Margaret Sangster.
Copy: DLC, PP.

270. "Descant"

WHEN SPRING COMES TRIP-PING OER THE   LEA

MS: Holograph called "When Spring Comes Tripping O'er the Lea," in col-
lection of PP.
Parts: Voice part only.
Pub: Cincinnati: John Church Co., 1901.
Text: Florence Earle Coates.
Agree: Agreement for royalty of 10 percent after first 200 copies. (Press-
er Documents.)
Misc: ARG listing, 1872 MS book.
Perf: ("Descant") MMS, December 21, 1898; "An Evening with the Song
Writers of Philadelphia," February 28, 1899, program noted that this was
the first public performance of the composition still in MS; Houston (Texas)
Symphony Club, February 24, 1908, sung by Mme. Zimmerman; MMS, Janu-
ary 23, 1918.
Copy: DLC.

271. "Dinkey Bird"

IN AN O-CEAN WAY OUT YON-DER

Pub: Philadelphia: Theodore Presser, 1899.
Text: Eugene Field.
Copy inf: Copyright renewed 1927 by Susan B. Gilchrist.
Agree: Added to Songs for the Children, March 1899. (Presser Documents.)
Price: $.20.
Royalty rate: $.03 per copy.
Royalties: September 1914, $1.02; September 1915, .48; September 1917, .24; September 1918, .30; 1920, .60; September 1921, .60.
Copy: Griffin collection, PP.

272. "Dirge for Summer, A"

ANDANTE

WEEP MOTH- ER NA-TURE WEEP! SUM-MER IS DEAD

Pub: New York: G. Schirmer, 1884.
Copy: DLC, NN, PP.

273. "Does He Love Me"

ALLEGRETTO

PRE-TTY RO- BIN AT MY WIN-DOW

Pub: Cincinnati: George D. Newhall, 1880.
Ded: Marian Fairlamb.
Misc: "Pretty Robin" in ARG listing.
Copy: LC.

274. "Down the Ages From Afar"

ALLEGRETTO

DOWN THE AGE-S FROM A FAR

MS: Autograph in collection of PP.
Parts: Soprano and piano.
Ocas. perf: Christmas.
Misc: Note on MS, "have but this one verse--should be others--don't remember source; perhaps it could be adapted to something else with more verses--same subject."

275. "Dream, Baby Dream"

Pub: New York: G. Schirmer, 1884.
Text: Barry Cornwall.
Ded: Mrs. A.H. Darling.
Copy: DLC, NN, PP.

276. "Dreaming"

MS: Holograph in collection of PP.

277. "Dreams"

Pub: Cincinnati: John Church Co., 1901.
Text: H.W. Raymond.
Agree: Agreement for royalty of 10 percent after first 20 copies. (Press-
er Documents.)
Copy: DLC.

278. "Drinking"

Pub: Philadelphia: William Wallace Gilchrist, 1886.
Copy inf: Copyright renewed 1914.

279. "Easter Song"

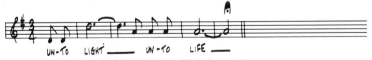

Pub: Philadelphia: William Wallace Gilchrist, 1878.
Text: M.H. Cobb.
Copy: DLC.

280. "Fairy and Child"

O LIS-TEN LIT-TLE DEAR MY SOUL TO THE FAIR-Y VOI-CES CALL-ING

Pub: Philadelphia: Theodore Presser, 1897.
Text: Eugene Field.
Agree: Added to Songs for the Children, February 1897. (Presser Documents.) Agreement for royalty of 15 percent after first 75 copies, March 1, 1897. (Presser Documents.)
Price: $.20.
Royalty rate: .03.
Royalties: September 1914, $.12; September 1918, .15; September 1922, 1.71; September 1923, .24; 1933, .03.
Perf: "An Evening with the Song Writers of Philadelphia," February 28, 1899.
Copy: Griffin collection, PP.

281. "Fairy Book"

WHEN MOTH-ER TAKES THE FAIR-Y BOOK

Pub: Educational Music Course. Boston: Ginn and Co., 1904.
Copy: DLC.

282. "Fiddle-dee-dee"

THERE ONCE WAS A BIRD THAT LIVED UP IN A TREE

Pub: Philadelphia: Theodore Presser, 1897.
Text: Eugene Field.
Agree: Added to Songs for the Children, February 1897. (Presser Documents.) Agreement for royalty of 15 percent after first 75 copies. (Ibid.)
Price: $.30.
Royalty rate: $.045 per copy.
Royalties: September 1914, $.09; September 1915, .54; 1920, .40; September 1921, .40.
Copy: Griffin collection, PP.

283. "Flag, The"

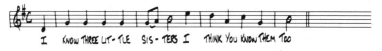

I KNOW THREE LIT-TLE SIS-TERS I THINK YOU KNOW THEM TOO

Pub: Songs for the Children. Philadelphia: Theodore Presser, 1897.
Text: E.L. McCord.
Copy: Griffin collection.

284. "Flow Down Cold Rivulet"

FLOW DOWN COLD RIV - U- LET

Pub: Boston: Arthur P. Schmidt, 1887.
Text: Tennyson.
Copy: DLC, NN, PP.

285. "Flower Seed"

ALLEGRETTO

FIRST A SEED SO TIN-Y   HID-DEN FROM THE SIGHT

Pub: Educational Music Course. Boston: Ginn and Co., 1904.
Copy: DLC.

286. "Flying Bird, The"

GRACEFULLY

FLY LIT-TLE BIRD IN GOLD - EN SUN

Pub: Songs for the Children. Philadelphia: Theodore Presser, 1899.
Copy: Griffin collection.

287. "Fountain, The"

IN-TO THE SUN-SHINE   FULL OF THE LIGHT

MS: Holograph in collection of PP.
Parts: Soprano and piano.
Text: J.R. Lowell.
Misc: Published by Presser for chorus of women's voices.

288. "From Far Away"

FROM FAR A -WAY WE COME TO YOU

Pub: New Hosanna. New York: New Church Board of Publication, 1902.
Ocas. perf: Christmas.
Copy: PBa.

289. "From Heaven Above"

Pub: Cincinnati: John Church Co., 1898.
Text: Martin Luther.
Agree: Assigned to John Church, April 20, 1898 for $40 with three other
songs. (Presser Documents. Other works were "All My Heart this Day
Rejoices," "Bethlehem," "Once in Royal David's City.") Published as
Three Carols for Christmas with "From Heaven Above," and "Once in Royal
David's City."
Copy: DLC, NN.

290. "Gingham Dog and Calico Cat, The"

Pub: Philadelphia: Theodore Presser, 1913.
Text: Eugene Field.
Copy inf: Copyright renewed 1927 by Susan B. Gilchrist.
Agree: Added to Songs for the Children, March 1899. (Ibid.)
Price: $.20.
Royalty rate: $.03 per copy.
Royalties: September 1914, $1.41; September 1915, 2.73; September 1917,
.99; September 1918, .84; September 1919, 1.75; 1920, 1.20; September
1921, 2.25; September 1922, 1.38; September 1923, 1.20; 1924 (21 copies
sold), .63; September 1925, .90; September 1927, .99; September 1928,
1.29; September 1929, 1.20; 1930, .36; September 1931, 1.44; 1933, .30;
September 1934, 14.20; September 1935, 11.30; 1936, 2.40; 1937, 3.90.
Copy: Griffin collection, PP.

291. "Going to the Fair"

Perf: At Song Recital by Camille Zeckwer, February 23, 1894.

292. "Golden Rod"

Pub: Boston: Arthur P. Schmidt, 1885.
Copy: DLC, NN, PP, PU.

293. "Gone Before"

MY SOUL IN SOR-ROW LAN-GUISH-ES

Pub: Boston: Oliver Ditson, 1892.
Text: William Wallace Gilchrist.
Copy: DLC.

294. "Good Christian People All"

GOOD CHRIST-IAN PEO-PLE ALL

Pub: Hosanna for Children. New York: New Church Board of Publication,
1905. Hosanna. New York: New Church Press, 1920.
Misc: Entered in Catalog of Copyright Entries, November 22, 1875.
Copy: CNJ (both books).

295. "Hast Thou a Song"

HAST THOU A SONG___ O SING-ER MINE

MS: Holograph in collection of PP.
Parts: Soprano and piano.
Misc: ARG listing, 1873 MS book.

296. "Hear O Shepherd of Israel"

HEAR O SHEP-HERD OF IS - RA - EL

MS: Holograph in collection of PP.
Parts: Recitative and aria for soprano and piano.
Text: From Psalm 80.
Misc: MS also for Two Serious Songs includes "Now and Afterwards" and
"Hear O Shepherd of Israel."

297. "Heart's Delight"

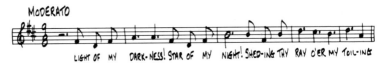

LIGHT OF MY   DARK-NESS! STAR OF MY   NIGHT! SHED-ING THY RAY O'ER MY TOIL-ING

Pub: New York: Edward Schuberth, 1886.
Text: W.W. Gilchrist.
Ded: Mr. Leonard Auty.
Copy inf: Copyright renewed 1914.
Perf: Grand Testimonial Concert, January 15, 1886; Musical Soirée at
Frankford Opera House (no longer in existence), February 2, 1888; Melody
Club, April 13, 1894; Testimonial Concert, May 21, 1914.
Copy: DLC, PP.

298. "Heaven and Earth Rejoice"

HEAV'N AND EARTH RE - JOICE ___

MS: Holograph in collection of PP.
Parts: Soprano and piano.
Pub: London: Weekes and Co., 1908.
Text: Arthur E. Stilwell.
Copy: LC.

299. "Here Awa', There Awa' (Wandering Willie)"

HERE A WA' THERE A WA' WAN-DER-ING WIL-LIE

Pub: Philadelphia: Theodore Presser, 1898.
Text: Robert Burns.
Copy inf: Copyright renewed 1928 by Susan B. Gilchrist.
Agree: Agreement for Six Scotch Songs, words by Robert Burns, October
29, 1897, no royalty on first 100 copies, 10 percent thereafter. (Presser
Documents.)
Price: $.30.
Royalty rate: .03.
Royalties: September 1915, $.14; September 1917, .36; September 1918,
.09; September 1919, 1.08.
Perf: MC, February 24, 1898; MMS, January 22, 1908; MC and MMS con-
cert, May 7, 1914; Testimonial Concert, May 21, 1914.
Copy: DLC, PP.

300. "Hills of Tennessee, The"

FAIR STAND THE HILLS OF TEN- NES- SEE

Pub: Philadelphia: Theodore Presser, 1899.
Text: Bushrod Washington James.
Copy: DLC.

301. "Hobby Horse"

HERE U- PON MY NO-BLE STEED UP AND DOWN UP AND DOWN

MS: Holograph in collection of PP.
Parts: Piano and voice.
Text: William Wallace Gilchrist.

302. "Home Sighs"

Agree: Assigned to John Church Co., Cincinnati, May 23, 1913 for $50
with two other songs. (Presser Documents. Other works were "Lullaby,"
"Summer's Evening.")

303. "How Many Thoughts"

HOW MAN-Y THOUGHTS I GIVE THEE   COME HERE U-PON THE GRASS

Pub: New York: G. Schirmer, 1884.
Parts: Soprano or tenor in F and mezzo-soprano or baritone in E^b.
Perf: Testimonial Concert, May 21, 1914; WPA program, May 21, 1937.
Copy: DLC, NN, PP. (all in E^b)

304. "Hunting Song"

ALLEGRO

RISE SLEEP NO MORE TIS A NO-BLE MORN

MS: Holograph in collection of PP.
Parts: Baritone voice and piano.
Text: Barry Cornwall.
Misc: ARG listing, published 1903. Note on MS, "get author words."
Agree: Assigned to John Church, February 16, 1894 for $50 with two

other songs. (Presser Documents. Other works were "Come See the
Place Where Jesus Lay," "The Sun and the Rosebud.")

305. "I Know a Maid"

Pub: New York: Edward Schuberth, 1886.
Copy inf: Copyright renewed 1914.
Copy: DLC.

306. "If Bluebirds Bloomed"

Perf: At Song Recital by Camille Zeckwer, February 23, 1894.

307. "In Love, If Love Be Love"

MS: Holograph in collection of PP.
Misc: One of four songs from Tennyson's Idylls of the King, song of
Vivian.

308. "In the Beginning Was the Word"

MS: Holograph in collection of PP.
Pub: Published by John Church for SATB, 1901.
Text: [Saint John.]

309. "In the Snowing and the Blowing"

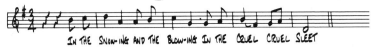

Pub: Songs for the Children. Philadelphia: Theodore Presser, 1897.
Text: M.M.D. [Mary Mapes Dodge.]
Copy: Griffin collection.

310. "In the Tree-Top"

Perf: At Song Recital by Camille Zeckwer, February 23, 1894.

311. "Into the Tomb of Ages Past"

SOLENELLE

IN-TO THE TOMBS OF AG-ES PAST   THE SO-LEMN YEARS ARE QUICK-LY CAST

Pub: New York: E.S. Lorenz, 1900.
Text: Penina Moses.
Copy: DLC.

312. "It Came Upon a Midnight Clear"

IT CAME U-PON THE MID-NIGHT CLEAR

Pub: New York: G. Schirmer, 1886.
Parts: Voice and organ.
Text: Edmund Hamilton Sears.
Copy: DLC.

313. "I've a Message"

I'VE A   MES-SAGE I'VE A   MES-SAGE

Pub: Educational Music Course. Boston: Ginn and Co., 1904.
Text: Mary Bailey.
Copy: DLC.

314. "Join Our Happy Carol"

Misc: Title listed on "It Came Upon a Midnight Clear," published by William H. Boner, Philadelphia.

315. "Joys of Spring (Concert Song for Soprano Voice)"

MODERATO

HENCE WITH ALL SOR-ROW AND TEARS___ AND ALL SIGH-ING

Pub: Philadelphia: Theodore Presser, 1897.
Copy inf: Copyright renewed 1924 by Susan B. Gilchrist.
Price: $.65.

Royalty rate: .0975.
Royalties: September 1918, $1.07; September 1919, 2.23; September 1921,
1.66; September 1922, 1.66; September 1923, 1.95; September 1932, .29.
Perf: The Wednesday Musical, December 16, 1896.
Copy: DLC, PP.

316. "King Death or the Coal Black Wine"

Pub: Philadelphia: G. Andre and Co., 1868.
Parts: Bass voice.
Text: Barry Cornwall.
Ded: Mr. W.H. Boner.
Copy: DLC, NN.

317. "Lamplighter"

Pub: Boston: Silver, Burdett and Co., 1912.
Text: David K. Stevens.

318. "Late, Late, So Late"

Pub: Boston: Oliver Ditson, 1908.
Text: Tennyson.
Misc: Published as Two Tennyson Songs with "Sweet is True Love."
Plates melted in 1921. (ARG ledger.) Originally planned as one of four
songs from Tennyson's Idylls of the King. Two were published, two are
in MS collection of FLP. Song of Guinevere.
Agree: Agreement for 10 percent royalty February 24, 1908. (Presser
Documents.)
Price: $.75.
Royalty rate: 10 percent.
Copy: DLC, PP.

319. "Life and Love"

MS: Holograph in collection of PP.
Parts: Piano and soprano parts in D major; A major piano part (notes for
voice indicated in spots, but no words), and a page called "Life" for so-

prano only in A major.
Text: Florence Earle Coates.

320. "Life's Mystery"

MS: Holograph, "We Are Born, We Laugh, We Weep," in E major in collec-
tion of PP. Two copies.
Pub: Philadelphia: Hatch Music Co., 1899.
Text: Thomas Moore.
Ded: Mr. Frank Cauffmann of Philadelphia.
Misc: ARG listing, 1872 MS book.
Copy: DLC.

321. "Lift the Heart, and Bend the Knee"

Misc: ARG listing, 1903.

322. "Lift Your Glad Voices"

Pub: New York: G. Schirmer, 1887.
Copy: DLC.

323. "Light of Light Enlighten Me"

Pub: New Hosanna. New York: New Church Board of Publication, 1902.
Hosanna. New York: New Church Press, 1920.
Copy: CNJ (Hosanna), PBa (New Hosanna).

324. "Little Boy Blue"

Pub: Songs for the Children. Philadelphia: Theodore Presser, 1897.
Text: [Mother Goose.]
Copy: Griffin collection.

325. "Little John Bottlejohn"

Perf: At Song Recital by Camille Zeckwer, February 23, 1894; MMS, November 29, 1916.

326. "Little Window, The"

Pub: Songs for the Children. Philadelphia: Theodore Presser, 1897.
Educational Music Course. Boston: Ginn and Co., 1904.
Text: Emily Huntington Miller.
Copy: Griffin collection (Songs for the Children), DLC (Educational Music Course).

327. "Long Wears the Day"

Pub: New York: Edward H. Phelps, 1892.
Parts: Alto voice.
Ded: Martha Barry.
Misc: Program note says song written in 1890.
Perf: Melody Club, April 31, 1894.
Copy: DLC, PP.

328. "Lord is My Shepherd, The"

Pub: Boston: C.C. Birchard and Co., 1909.
Text: Psalm 23.

329. "Lost"

Pub: Boston: Arthur P. Schmidt, 1885.
Copy: DLC.

330. "Lost Voice, The"

Pub: Cincinnati: George D. Newhall, 1882.
Text: Mrs. J.R. Fairlamb.
Copy: DLC.

331. "Love Song, A"

Pub: Boston: Arthur P. Schmidt, 1885.
Text: Barry Cornwall.
Copy: DLC, NN.

332. "Love's Beginning"

Pub: Boston: Arthur P. Schmidt, 1887.
Text: Barry Cornwall.
Copy: DLC, NN, PP.

333. "Loving Saviour, Friend So Dear"

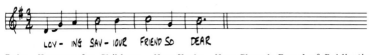

Pub: Hosanna for Children. New York: New Church Board of Publication,
1905.
Copy: CNJ.

334. "Lullaby"

Pub: Songs for the Children. Philadelphia: Theodore Presser, 1897.
Copy: Griffin collection.

335. "Lullaby (Softly in the Summer Air)"

SOFT-LY THE   SUM-MER AIR WITH BAL-MY O-DORS LA-DEN

Pub: Philadelphia: Theodore Presser, 1893. Favorite Masterpieces.
Edited by Dressler. New York: The Standard Musical Association, 1897.
Text: W.W. Gilchrist.
Ded: Margaretta.
Agree: Agreement June 23, 1911: Gilchrist gave plates to Presser as
custodian to produce copies as demand required; royalty of 15 percent.
(Presser Documents.) Agreement May 23, 1913 with John Church for $50.
(Ibid.)
Royalty rate: $.06.
Royalties: September 1915, $1.14; September 1917, .60; September 1918,
1.20; September 1921, .30; September 1928, 1.14; 1933, .30; 1937, .30.
Perf: MMS, April 17, 1895; Melusine Club, May 17, 1899.
Copy: DLC, NN (sheet and Favorite Masterpieces).

336. "Madrigal"

Perf: Tenor solo performed at MC concert, February 24, 1898.

337. "March, A"

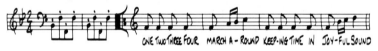

ONE TWO THREE FOUR   MARCH A-ROUND KEEP-ING TIME IN JOY-FUL SOUND

Pub: Philadelphia: Theodore Presser, 1900.
Copy inf: Copyright renewed 1928 by Susan B. Gilchrist.
Agree: Added to Songs for the Children, October 13, 1898. (Ibid.)
Royalty rate: $.0225 per copy.
Royalties: September 1915, $.07.
Copy: Griffin collection.

338. "Maud"

Misc: Listed in ARG ledger, published by Theodore Presser, Philadelphia.
Price: $.15.
Royalty rate: $.0225 per copy.

339. "Meadow Talk"

ALLEGRETTO

A BUM-BLE BEE YEL-LOW AS GOLD___ SAT PERCHED ON A RED CLO-VER TOP

Pub: <u>Songs for the Children</u>. Philadelphia: Theodore Presser, 1897.
Text: Caroline Leslie.
Perf: MMS, November 29, 1916.
Copy: Griffin collection.

340.   "Merry Christmas Bells Are Ringing"

Pub: <u>A Liturgy for the General Church of the New Jerusalem</u>. Bryn
Athyn, Pa., 1966 edition. <u>Hosanna</u>. New York: New Church Press, 1920.
<u>Hosanna</u>. revised edition. Boston: The Swedenborg Press, 1968.
Misc: Entered in Catalog of Copyright Entries, November 22, 1875.
Copy: CNJ (<u>Hosanna</u>, both editions), PBa (<u>A Liturgy for the General
Church of the New Jerusalem</u>).

341.   "Morning Hymn"

Pub: <u>Songs for the Children</u>. Philadelphia: Theodore Presser, 1897.
<u>Educational Music Course</u>. Boston: Ginn and Co., 1904.
Copy: DLC (<u>Educational Music Course</u>), Griffin collection (<u>Songs for the
Children</u>).

342.   "Mother's Song"

Pub: Philadelphia: Theodore Presser, 1897. <u>Songs for the Children</u>.
Philadelphia: Theodore Presser, 1897.
Agree: Added to <u>Songs for the Children</u>, February 1897. (Presser Docu-
ments.)
Price: $.20.
Royalty rate: $.03 per copy.
Royalties: September 1918, $.39; 1920, .36; September 1921, .57; Septem-
ber 1928, .24.
Copy: Griffin collection (<u>Songs for the Children</u>), PP (sheet).

343.   "My Dream"

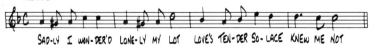

Pub: Philadelphia: Theodore Presser, 1897.
Copy inf: Copyright renewed 1924 by Susan B. Gilchrist.
Royalty rate: $.1125 per copy.
Royalties: September 1917, $.90.
Perf: MMS, May 22, 1895.
Copy: DLC, PP.

344. "My Heart is Sair"

ANDANTE

MY HEART IS SAIR I DARE NOT TELL MY HEART IS SAIR FOR SOME-BO-DY

Pub: New York: G. Schirmer, 1895.
Text: Robert Burns.
Copy inf: Copyright renewed 1923 by ARG.
Misc: Published as Three Scotch Songs with "The Blue-eyed Lassie," and
"Dainty Davie."
Perf: Song Recital by Edward M. Zimmerman, June 14, 1897; Philadelphia
Composers' Concert, January 29, 1898.
Copy: DLC.

345. "My Highland Lassie, O"

ALLEGRETTO

NAE GEN-TLE DAMES THOUGH E'ER SAY FAIR

Pub: Philadelphia: Theodore Presser, 1898.
Text: Robert Burns.
Copy inf: Copyright renewed 1928 by Susan B. Gilchrist.
Agree: Agreement for Six Scotch Songs, words by Robert Burns, October
29, 1897, no royalties on first 100 copies, 10 percent thereafter. (Presser
Documents.)
Price: $.30.
Royalty rate: .03.
Royalties: September 1918, $.30; September 1921, .30; September 1923,
.15; September 1925, .57; September 1928, .63.
Copy: DLC.

346. "My Ladye"

ALLEGRETTO

IN HER GAR-DEN COOL AND SHA-DY

Pub: Cincinnati: John Church Co., 1902.
Text: Baroness de Bertarech.
Copy inf: Copyright renewed 1928.
Agree: Agreement for royalty of 10 percent after first 200 copies. (Ibid.)
Perf: MMS, November 18, 1896; MMS, November 19, 1916.
Copy: DLC.

347. "My Sins! My Sins! My Saviour"

Pub: Philadelphia: Geibel and Lehman, 1905.
Text: J.B. Monsell.
Copy inf: Copyright renewed 1933 by Susan B. Gilchrist.
Misc: Number one in F minor, number two in C minor.
Perf: Testimonial Concert, May 21, 1914.
Copy: DLC, PP (both in C minor).

348. "My Soul is Dark"

Pub: Milwaukee: William Rohlfing, 1891.
Text: Lord Byron.
Copy: DLC.

349. "Nature's Lullaby (To Anna)"

Pub: Philadelphia: Theodore Presser, 1893.
Text: W.W. Gilchrist.
Ded: Anna [Gilchrist].
Agree: Agreement June 23, 1911: Gilchrist gave plates to Presser as custodian to produce copies as demand required; royalty of 15 percent. (Presser Documents.)
Royalty rate: $.0750 per copy.
Royalties: September 1915, $.75; September 1917, .60; September 1918, 1.20; September 1920, 2.10.
Copy: DLC, PP.

350. "New Jerusalem, The"

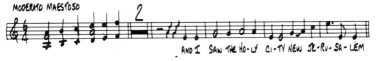

Pub: New York: G. Schirmer, 1906.
Text: From the Revelation, hymn from English confesisonal.
Misc: Published for high voice in C, medium in B♭, low in A♭.
Price: $.75.

Royalty rate: 10 percent.
Royalties: high: February 1913, $.82; 1914, .52; 1915, .67; 1916, .22;
1919, .30; February 1923, .68; February 1924, .68; February 1925, .60;
February 1926, .52; February 1927, 4 copies sold for 3.00; 1929, 4 copies
sold for 3.00; February 1930, 5 copies sold for 3.75; medium: 1915, .22;
1916, .67; 1917, .60; 1918, 1.12; February 1930, 4 copies sold for 3.00;
low: February 1913, 1.87; 1914, .15; 1916, .23; February 1925, .90;
February 1926, .30; February 1927, 10 copies sold for 7.50; 1929, 10 copies
sold for 7.50.
Copy: DLC, NN, PP (all in C).

351. "New Year's Day"

Pub: Hosanna for Children. New York: New Church Board of Publication,
1905.
Copy: CNJ.

352. "Nightfall"

Misc: ARG listing, 1871 MS book.

353. "Nocturne"

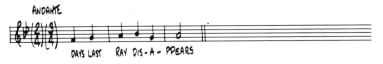

MS: Holograph in collection of PP.
Parts: Soprano and piano.
Misc: Written in alternating measures of 2/4 and 3/4. Note at bottom "The
measures to be of equal duration."

354. "Now and Afterward"

MS: Holograph in collection of PP.
Parts: Soprano and piano.
Text: Miss Muloch.
Misc: MS is for Two Serious Songs with "Hear, O Shepherd of Israel."

355. "Now to Heaven Our Prayer Ascending"

Copy inf: Entered in Catalog of Copyright Entries, May 23, 1902.

356. "O Little Town of Bethlehem"

Pub: New York: G. Schirmer, 1905.
Parts: Medium voice with organ.
Text: Phillips Brooks.
Ocas. perf: Christmas hymn.
Copy inf: Entered in Catalog of Copyright Entries, July 5, 1902. Copy-
right renewed 1933 by ARG.
Price: $.60.
Royalties: February 1913, $.45; 1914, .75; 1915, 2.80; 1916, .65; Febru-
ary 1922, 5.15; February 1925, 3.95; February 1927, 7.70; February 1928,
57 sold but deducted on account of return of stock; 1930, 23.40.
Copy: DLC, PP.

357. "O Look at the Moon"

Pub: Songs for the Children. Philadelphia: Theodore Presser, 1897.
Text: Mrs. Follen.
Copy: Griffin collection.

358. "O Lord, Thou Hast Searched Me Out"

Pub: New York: G. Schirmer, 1906.
Text: From Psalm 139.
Misc: High and low voices.
Price: $.75.
Royalty rate: 10 percent.
Royalties: low voice: February 1913, $8.40; 1914, 5.85; 1915, 4.20; 1916,
4.05; 1917, 1.95; 1918, 1.88; 1919, 3.67; February 1921, 1.88; February
1922, 1.88; February 1923, 2.93; February 1924, 3.38; February 1925,
2.25; February 1926, 1.05; 1927, 19 copies sold for 14.25; February 1928,
29 copies sold for 21.75; 1929, 20 copies sold for 15.00; 1930, 30 copies
sold for 22.50; high voice: February 1913, 8.40; 1914, 5.85; 1915, 4.20;
1916, 4.05; 1917, 1.95; 1918, 1.88; 1919, 3.67; February 1921, 1.88; February 1922, 1.88; February 1923, 2.93; February 1924, 3.38; February
1925, 2.25; February 1928, 1.05; 1927, 19 copies sold for 14.25; February
1928, 29 copies sold for 21.75; 1929, 20 copies sold for 15.00; 1930, 30
copies sold for 22.50.
Perf: Testimonial Concert, May 21, 1914.
Copy: DLC, PP (both in F).

359. "O Many and Many a Year Ago"

Pub: New York: G. Schirmer, 1880.
Text: M.H. Cobb.
Ocas. perf: Christmas song.
Copy: DLC.

360. "O My Luve's Like the Red, Red Rose"

Pub: Philadelphia: Theodore Presser, 1898.
Text: Robert Burns.
Agree: Agreement for Six Scotch Songs, words by Robert Burns, October
29, 1897, no royalty on first 100 copies, 10 percent thereafter. (Presser
Documents.)
Perf: MMS, April 28, 1897.
Copy: LC.

361. "O Star of Bethlehem"

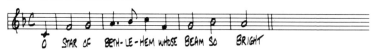

Pub: New York: G. Schirmer, 1886.
Ocas. perf: Christmas Carol.
Copy inf: Copyright renewed 1914.
Copy: DLC.

362. "O'er the Hill and O'er the Vale"

Pub: Hosanna for Children. New York: New Church Board of Publication,
1905.
Copy: CNJ.

363. "Oh, My Laddie's Gone Away"

Pub: Boston: Oliver Ditson, 1908.
Text: W.W. Gilchrist.
Misc: Plates melted 1914. (ARG ledger.)
Agree: Agreement February 24, 1908, 10 percent royalty. (Presser Documents.)
Price: $.60.
Royalty rate: 10 percent.
Royalties: January 1917, $.60; January 1919, .30; July 1921, .30.
Copy: DLC, PP.

364. "Oh, Wert Thou in the Cauld Blast"

Pub: Philadelphia: Theodore Presser, 1898.
Text: Robert Burns.
Copy inf: Copyright renewed 1926 by Susan B. Gilchrist.
Agree: Agreement for Six Scotch Songs, words by Robert Burns, October 29, 1897, no royalty on first 100 copies, 10 percent thereafter. (Ibid.)
Price: $.25.
Royalty rate: $.0250 per copy.
Royalties: September 1917, $.03; September 1922, .32.
Copy: DLC.

365. "Oh Wert Thou in the Cauld Blast"

MS: Holographs in collection of PP, one in F major, one in E♭.

366. "Old Mother Hubbard"

 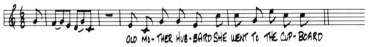

Pub: Songs for the Children. Philadelphia: Theodore Presser, 1897.
Copy: Griffin collection.

367.   "On the Mountain Top Appearing"

MS: Holograph in collection of PP.
Parts: Soprano and piano.
Text: Rev. W. Kelley, 1802.

368.   "Once in Royal David's City"

Pub: Cincinnati: John Church Co., 1898.
Text: Cecil Alexander.
Misc: Published as Three Carols for Christmas with "All My Heart This
Day Rejoices," and "From Heaven Above."
Agree: Assigned to John Church, April 20, 1898 for $40 with three other
songs. (Presser Documents. Other songs were "All My Heart This Day
Rejoices," "Bethlehem," "From Heaven Above.")
Copy: DLC, NN.

369.   "Once There Was a Little Voice"

Pub: Boston: Arthur P. Schmidt, 1887.
Copy: DLC, NN, PP.

370.   "Our Country Friends"

MS: Holograph dated "Xmass '92," inscribed "A Kid's Song from Doodles,"
in Gilchrist scrapbook. (Gilchrist's children called him "Doodles" when they
were young.)
Pub: Songs for the Children. Philadelphia: Theodore Presser, 1897.
Copy: Griffin collection.

371. "Paper Soldiers' Brigade, The"

MARCH TIME

MANY A WEA-RY MARCH AND LONG

Ms: Autograph in collection of PP.
Parts: Voice and piano.
Text: W.W. Gilchrist.
Misc: Three verses of poetry written on front cover.

372. "Parted Friends"

Misc: ARG listing date 1867, publisher C.W.A. Trumpler.

373. "Parting (Ballad for Alto)"

MODERATO

LONG SHA-DOWS TELL OF DAY'S DE-CLIN-ING.

Pub: Philadelphia: Theodore Presser, 1893.
Agree: Agreement June 23, 1911: Gilchrist gave plates to Presser as
custodian to produce copies as demand required; royalty of 15 percent.
(Presser Documents.)
Royalty rate: $.06 per copy.
Royalties: September 1915, $1.14; September 1917, .60; September 1918,
1.20; September 1921, .42; September 1928, 1.14.
Copy: DLC.

374. "Passing"

PASS-ING OUT OF THE SHA-DOW IN-TO A PUR-ER LIGHT

Pub: Cincinnati: John Church Co., 1901.
Text: Baroness de Bertarech.
Agree: Agreement for royalty of 10 percent after first 200 copies. (Ibid.)
Copy: DLC.

375. "Peace on Earth"

WITH SPIRIT

SING "PEACE ON EARTH GOOD WILL TO MEN" THE AN-GELS SONG RE-PEAT

MS: Holograph in collection of PP.
Parts: Soprano and piano.

164   William Wallace Gilchrist

376. "Piper, The"

ALLEGRETTO SEMPLICE

PIP-ING DOWN THE   VAL-LEY WILD

MS: Holograph in collection of PP.
Parts: Soprano and piano.
Text: Blake.

377. "Points of the Compass, The"

TO THE   NORTH-WARD   POINT

Pub: Songs for the Children. Philadelphia: Theodore Presser, 1897.
Copy: Griffin collection.

378. "Poor Love"

Perf: MMS, December 22, 1902.

379. "Poor Wounded Heart"

ANDANTE

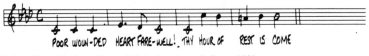

POOR WOUN-DED HEART FARE-WELL! THY HOUR OF   REST IS COME

Pub: New York: Edward Schuberth and Co., 1891.
Text: Barry Cornwall.
Copy: DLC, PP.

380. "Prayers of Love"

ANDANTE

PRAYERS OF   LOVE   LIKE   RAIN- DROPS   FALL

MS: Holograph in collection of PP.
Parts: Soprano and piano.
Text: John G. Whither.

381. "Prince of Galilee, The"

THE WISE MEN ONCE BE-HELD A STAR

Pub: London: Novello and Co., Ltd., 1906.
Text: A.E. Stilwell.
Copy: DLC.

382. "Quiet"

SOUL BE QUI-ET BET-TER SHALT THOU SEE

Pub: Boston: Arthur P. Schmidt, 1885.
Perf: MMS, November 15, 1899.
Copy: LC, FLP.

383. "Raise We Now Our Hearts and Voices"

Pub: New York: William A. Pond and Co., 1887.
Ocas. perf: Christmas Carol.
Copy: DLC (listed in catalog, but not located in collection).

384. "Recessional"

GOD OF OUR FA-THERS KNOWN OF OLD

Pub: New York: G. Schirmer, 1902.
Text: Rudyard Kipling.
Copy inf: Copyright renewed 1929.
Copy: DLC, PP.

385. "Recitative and Aria"

Perf: MMS, January 19, 1898.

386. "Regrets, or Far So Far"

FLOW'RS THAT MY GAR-DEN DE- LIGHT- ED   FLOW'RS THAT MY GAR-DEN DE - LIGHT- ED

MS: Holographs in collection of PP.
Parts: Soprano and piano.
Misc: One copy in F minor, two in A minor.
Perf: MMS, January 19, 1898.

387. "Reign of Peace, The"

FROM NORTH TO   SOUTH THE AN - THEM   RING

Pub: Philadelphia: Theodore Presser, 1898.
Text: Bushrod Washington James.
Price: $.30.
Royalty rate: $.03 per copy.
Royalties: September 1921, $.45.
Copy: DLC, PP.

388. "Rest"

Misc: ARG listing, 1867 MS book.

389. "Reverie"

Pub: Milwaukee: William Rohlfing, 1891.
Parts: Baritone solo with 'cello obligato.
Text: W.W. Gilchrist.
Perf: Testimonial Concert, May 21, 1914.

390. "Ring Out Ye Bells So Cheerily"

Misc: Title listed on "Raise We Now Our Hearts and Voices," published
William A. Pond, New York.

391. "Ring Out Wild Bells"

RING OUT WILD BELLS TO THE WILD SKY

Pub: New Hosanna. New York: New Church Board of Publication, 1902.
Hosanna. New York: New Church Press, 1920.
Text: Tennyson.
Copy: CNJ (Hosanna), PBa (New Hosanna).

392. "Rippling, Purling Little River"

Pub: Songs for the Children. Philadelphia: Theodore Presser, 1897.
Text: Lucy Larcom.
Copy: Griffin collection.

393. "Robin's Journey, The"

Pub: Educational Music Course. Boston: Ginn and Co., 1904.
Text: Celia Standish.

394. "Rock-A-Bye Baby"

Pub: Songs for the Children. Philadelphia: Theodore Presser, 1897.
Text: [Mother Goose.]
Copy: Griffin collection.

395. "Rock-A-By Lady, The"

Pub: Songs of Childhood. Edited by Reginald DeKoven. New York:
Charles Scribners' Sons, 1896.
Text: Eugene Field.
Copy: DLC.

396. "Rolling On"

Misc: ARG listing, 1872 MS book.

397. "Roseate Hues of Early Dawn, The"

Pub: New York: G. Schirmer, 1906.
Text: Cecil F. Alexander.
Copy inf: Copyright renewed 1934 by ARG.
Misc: High and low voices with organ accompaniment.
Price: $.60.
Royalty rate: 10 percent.
Royalties: high: February 1913, $2.58; 1914, .60; 1915, .90; 1916, .12;
1917, 1.08; 1924, .36; 1927, 18 copies sold for 10.80.
Copy: DLC, PP (both in E^b).

398. "Row Gently Here My Gondolier"

MS: Holograph in collection of PP.
Parts: Soprano and piano.
Text: Thomas Moore.
Misc: Music in 12/8. Two copies. Note on copy one, "Music by Roman-
ticist."

399. "Sea! The Sea!, The"

MS: Holograph in collection of PP.
Parts: Soprano and piano.
Text: Barry Cornwall.
Misc: ARG listing, 1869 MS book.

400. "See the Lilies"

Pub: New Hosanna. New York: New Church Board of Publication, 1902.
Ocas. perf: Flower day.
Copy: PBa.

401. "Seed Babies"

Pub: <u>Songs for the Children</u>. Philadelphia: Theodore Presser, 1897.
Text: E.L. McCord.
Copy: Griffin collection.

402. "Serenade (I dream of thee)"

MS: Holograph in collection of PP.
Parts: Soprano and keyboard.
Pub: Philadelphia: Theodore Presser, 1897.
Copy inf: Copyright renewed 1924 by Susan B. Gilchrist.
Price: $.50.
Royalty rate: $.075 per copy.
Royalties: 1913, $.37; September 1914, .68; September 1915, 1.28; September 1917, .53; September 1923, .23; 1927, .75; 1933, .37.
Copy: DLC, PP.

403. "She's a Winsome Wee Thing"

Pub: Philadelphia: Theodore Presser, 1898.
Text: Robert Burns.
Copy inf: Copyright renewed 1923 by Susan B. Gilchrist.
Agree: Agreement for <u>Six Scotch Songs</u>, words by Robert Burns, October 29, 1897, no royalty on first 100 copies, 10 percent thereafter. (Presser Documents.)
Copy: DLC, PP.

404. "Shout the News to Every Nation"

Misc: Title listed on "It Came Upon a Midnight Clear," published by William H. Boner, Philadelphia.

405. "Sick Bird"

Poor little Dic-ky Bird Droop-ing A-gain   Poor lit-tle Dic-ky Bird where is your Pain?

Pub: Philadelphia: Theodore Presser, 1899.
Text: W.W. Gilchrist.
Copy inf: Copyright renewed 1927 by Susan B. Gilchrist.
Agree: Added to Songs for the Children, March 1899. (Presser Documents).
Price: $.40.
Royalty rate: $.06 per copy.
Royalties: September 1914, $.18; September 1915, .06; September 1918,
.12; 1920, .20; September 1921, .60; September 1928, 1.08; 1933, .30.
Copy: PP.

406. "Sing 'Peace on Earth'"

Misc: ARG listing, Christmas.

407. "Sing! Sing!"

ALLEGRO

Sing! Sing! Mu-sic was gi-ven to brigh-ten the gay.

Pub: New York: G. Schirmer, 1884.
Parts: Soprano or tenor in D, alto or baritone in C.
Text: Barry Cornwall.
Ded: Mr. W.H. Becket.
Copy: DLC, NN, PP (all in D).

408. "Skylark, The"

ALLEGRETTO

Bird of the wil-der-ness Blithe-some and cum-ber-less

Pub: Fifth Music Reader. Boston: Ginn and Co., 1906.
Text: James Hogg.
Copy: DLC.

409. "Slumber Song"

ANDANTE

O Blue eyes close in slum-ber O Bird-ie on your nest

Pub: Educational Music Course. Boston: Ginn and Co., 1904.

Text: Caris Brook.
Copy: DLC.

410.   "Snowfall"

THIS IS THE WAY THE SNOW COMES DOWN

Pub: Hosanna for Children.   New York: New Church Board of Publication,
1905.   Hosanna.   New York: New Church Board of Publication, 1968.
Copy: CNJ (both books).

411.   "Softly the Echoes Come and Go"

SOFT-LY THE EC- HOES COME AND GO___   OV-ER THE CRACKLING FROST AND SNOW

Pub: New York: G. Schirmer, 1883.   Hosanna for Children.   New York:
New Church Board of Publication, 1905.
Ocas. perf: Christmas.
Copy: CNJ (Hosanna for Children), DLC (sheet), NN (sheet).

412.   "Soldier of Love"

LOVE CALLS IN   MA-NY TONES AND   MAN FLIES TO MEET HER

MS: Holograph in collection of PP.
Parts: Soprano and piano.
Text: W.W. Gilchrist.

413.   "Soldier's Departure"

GO FETCH TO ME A PINT OF WINE AND FILL IT IN A SIL-VER TAS-SIE

Pub: Philadelphia: Hatch Music Co., 1908.
Text: Robert Burns.
Copy: DLC, PP.

172   William Wallace Gilchrist

414. "Something I May Not Win"

SOME-THING I   MAY NOT WIN

MS: Autograph in collection of PP.
Parts: Soprano and piano.

415. "Song of Doubt and a Song of Faith, A"

THE DAY IS QUENCHED AND THE SUN IS FLED   GOD HAS FOR-GOT-TEN THE WORLD

DAY WILL RE- TURN WITH A   FRESH-ER BOON

Pub: New York: G. Schirmer, 1884.
Text: George Holland.
Ded: S.D.D.
Perf: MMS, November 15, 1899.
Copy: DLC, NN, PP.

416. "Song of Life"

Perf: MMS, December 22, 1902.

417. "Song of the Wave"

OUR FA-THER MAKES EACH PRE-TTY CLOUD THAT SAILS A - LONG ____THE SKY

Pub: [n.p.]: M.G. Kennedy, 1898.
Text: Francis Chadwick.
Copy: DLC.

418. "Sound Over All Waters"

SOUND O-VER ALL   WA-TERS REACH OUT FROM ALL   LANDS

Pub: New Hosanna. New York: New Church Board of Publication, 1902.
A Liturgy for the General Church of the New Jerusalem. Bryn Athyn,
Pa.: Academy Book Room, 1908, 1916 editions.
Text: John G. Whittier.
Ocas. perf: Christmas.
Copy: PBa (all books).

419. "Southern Lullaby"

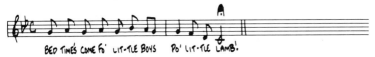

BED TIME'S COME Fo' LIT-TLE BOYS   Po' LIT-TLE LAMB!

Pub: Philadelphia: Theodore Presser, 1897.
Text: Paul Lawrence Dunbar.
Agree: Agreement April 8, 1897 for 10 percent royalty after first 75
copies sold. (Presser Documents.)
Royalty rate: $.03 per copy.
Royalties: September 1914, $.21; September 1915, .21; September 1917,
.27; September 1929, .65; September 1931, .18; September 1932, .12.
Perf: MMS, April 20, 1898.
Copy: DLC, PP.

420. "Spring"

ALL THE DEAR BIRD-IES ARE WITH US A - GAIN   OUT IN THE OR-CHARD TO - DAY

Pub: Songs for the Children. Philadelphia: Theodore Presser, 1897.
Copy: Griffin collection.

421. "Spring Grasses"

Perf: December 28, 1945 by Gertrude Traubel.

422. "Spring's Awakening"

MY HEART TO THE HEA-VENS UP- RIS-ING

MS: Holograph in collection of PP.
Misc: Note on MS, "Song for baritone or contralto," and piano.

423. "Star, The"

THERE'S A TWINK-LING LIT-TLE STAR O! So   HIGH O! So   HIGH

Pub: Songs for the Children. Philadelphia: Theodore Presser, 1897.
Text: W.W. Gilchrist.
Copy: Griffin collection.

424. "Stars"

O-VER OUR HEADS ON THE ROOF OF THE SKY

Pub: Educational Music Course. Boston: Ginn and Co., 1904.
Text: Nathan Haskell Dole.
Copy: DLC.

425. "Stop, Stop, Pretty Water"

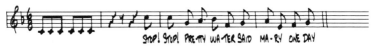

STOP! STOP! PRETTY WA-TER SAID MA-RY ONE DAY

Pub: Songs for the Children. Philadelphia: Theodore Presser, 1897.
Copy: Griffin collection.

426. "Summer's Evening"

Agree: Assigned to John Church Co., May 23, 1913 for $50 with two other songs. (Presser Documents. Other songs were "Home Sighs" and "Lullaby.")

427. "Sun and the Rosebud, The"

THE SUN WHO SMILES WHERE-EV-ER HE GOES TILL THE FLO-WERS ALL SMILE A-GAIN

Pub: Cincinnati: John Church Co., 1894.
Text: Alice Carey.
Agree: Assigned to John Church Co., February 16, 1894 for $50 with two other songs. (Presser Documents. Other songs were "Come See the Place Where Jesus Lay," and "Hunting Song.")
Copy: DLC.

428. "Sweet is True Love"

SWEET IS TRUE BLUE   THO' GIV'N IN VAIN IN VAIN —

Pub: Boston: Oliver Ditson, 1908.
Text: Tennyson.
Misc: Published as Two Tennyson Songs with "Late, Late, So Late."
Originally planned as one of four songs from Tennyson's Idylls of the King. Two were published, two are in MS collection of PP. Song of Elaine.
Agree: Agreement for 10 percent royalty February 24, 1908. (Ibid.)
Price: $.60.

Royalty rate: 10 percent.
Royalties: January 1917, $1.80; July 1917, .60; July 1918, 1.80; 1927, .30.
Perf: Program of the National Federation of Musical Clubs Seventh Biennial Festival and Convention, March 30, 1911; MMS, November 29, 1916.
Copy: DLC, PP.

429. "Sweetheart"

Pub: Philadelphia: William H. Boner, 1874.
Copy: PP.

430. "Te Dominum"

Copy inf: Entered in Catalog of Copyright Entries, March 20, 1901.

431. "There's A Song in the Air"

Ocas. perf: Christmas Song.
Copy inf: Entered in Catalog of Copyright Entries, May 26, 1902.

432. "Thou'rt Like Unto a Flower"

Pub: Cincinnati: John Church Co., 1901.
Text: Heine.
Agree: Agreement for 10 percent royalty after 200 copies; listed as "Du bist wie eine Blume." (Presser Documents.)
Perf: MMS, January 28, 1902; Testimonial Concert, May 21, 1914; MC Fortieth Anniversary Concert, April 14, 1915.
Copy: DLC.

433. "Three Little Kittens"

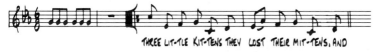

Pub: Philadelphia: Theodore Presser, 1897. Songs for the Children.
Philadelphia: Theodore Presser, 1897.
Text: [Author of words unknown, attributed to Elizabeth Lee Follen and to Eliza Cook.]
Agree: Added to Songs for the Children, February 1897. (Ibid.) Agree-

ment for royalty of 15 percent after first 75 copies, March 1, 1897. (Presser Documents.)

Price: $.30.

Royalty rate: $.045 per copy.

Royalties: September 1914, $.54; September 1915, .95; September 1917, .63; September 1918, .67; 1920, 2.75; 1924, 22 copies sold, .99; September 1929, .09; September 1931, .86; 1933, .13.

Copy: Griffin collection (Songs for the Children).

434. "Time's Cure"

MS: Autograph in collection of PP.

Parts: Soprano and piano.

435. "To the Moon"

MS: Holograph in collection of PP.

Parts: Soprano and organ or piano.

Text: Shelley.

Misc: Note on MS, "to illustrate minor scale."

436. "Turn, Fortune, Turn Thy Wheel"

MS: Autograph in collection of PP.

Parts: Soprano and piano.

Misc: One of four songs from Tennyson's Idylls of the King. Song of Enid.

437. "Twilight Song"

MS: Holograph in collection of PP.

Parts: Soprano and piano, four hands.

Ded: Mr. S.D. Smith of Philadelphia.

Misc: ARG listing, 1869 MS book.

438. "Two Villages, The"

Pub: New York: G. Schirmer, 1884.
Text: [Rose Terry Cooke.]
Ded: Mrs. C.L. Yarnall.
Copy: DLC, NN, PP.

439. "Under the Greenwood Tree"

Misc: ARG listing, 1903.

440. "Violet, The"

Misc: ARG listing, 1913 MS book.

441. "Voice of the Sea, The"

Pub: Boston: Arthur P. Schmidt, 1885.
Text: T.B. Aldrich.
Perf: Song Recital by Camille Zeckwer, December 20, 1894.
Copy: DLC, MH, NN.

442. "Wae Is My Heart"

Pub: Philadelphia: Hatch Music Co., 1908.
Text: Robert Burns.
Copy: DLC.

443. "Wallace"

Pub: Magnificat. New York: New Church Board of Publication, 1910.
Text: C.E. Rowe.
Copy: CNJ.

444. "Waves of the Far Away Ocean"

Pub: Boston: Arthur P. Schmidt, 1885.
Perf: MMS, April 28, 1897.
Copy: DLC, NN, PU.

445. "When Thou Art Nigh"

Pub: Philadelphia: William H. Boner, 1874.
Ded: "To My Wife."
Copy: DLC, PP.

446. "When Twilight Dews"

Pub: Milwaukee: William Rohlfing, 1891.
Text: Thomas Moore.
Misc: 'Cello obligato.
Copy: DLC, PP.

447. "Where E'er I Wander"

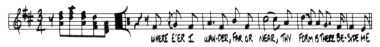

Pub: Boston: Oliver Ditson, 1892.
Text: William Wallace Gilchrist.
Copy: DLC.

448. "Where Would I Be (A Sea Song)"

Pub: Boston: Oliver Ditson, 1893.
Text: W.W. Gilchrist.
Price: $.50.
Perf: Testimonial to Miss Emma Miller, December 3, 1897.
Copy: DLC, PP.

449. "While Shepherds Watched Their Flocks by Night"

Pub: Philadelphia: Theodore Presser, 1901.
Text: Nahum Tate.
Agree: Agreement November 11, 1901, 10 percent royalty after first 75
copies. (Presser Documents.)
Price: $.40.
Royalty rate: $.06 per copy.
Royalties: September 1918, $.18; September 1919, .60; 1920, 2.40; Septem-
ber 1921, 2.28; September 1923, .84; September 1924, 2.16; September
1927, 1.56; September 1928, .60; September 1929, .84.
Copy: PP.

450. "Why Shines the Moon So Dim"

Pub: New York: Edward Schuberth, 1891.
Perf: MMS, December 21, 1898.
Copy: DLC, PP.

451. "Widow Bird"

MS: Holograph in collection of PP.
Parts: Soprano and piano.
Text: [Shelley.]
Misc: Note on MS, "Forget where words come from--think Keats or
Nord...."

452. "Wildflower, The"

TWAS IN A FOR-EST AB - SORB'D IN THOUGHT

Pub: <u>Fourth Music Reader</u>. Boston: Ginn and Co., 1905.
Copy: DLC.

453. "With Bitter Grief My Heart is Aching"

ANDANTE

WITH BIT-TER GRIEF MY HEART IS   ACH - ING

MS: Holograph in collection of PP.
Parts: Soprano and piano.
Misc: ARG listing date, 1872.

454. "Woodman, The"

BRISKLY

THE WOOD-MAN CUTS THE FOR-EST TREE THE SAW-YER MADE THESE BOARDS YOU SEE

Pub: <u>Songs for the Children</u>. Philadelphia: Theodore Presser, 1897.
Text: Sophia Bixby.
Copy: Griffin collection.

455. "Wynken, Blynken and Nod"

WYN-KEN AND BLYN-KEN AND NOD ONE NIGHT

MS: Holograph in collection of PP.
Parts: Incomplete voice part only for part of each of four verses.
Pub: Philadelphia: Theodore Presser, 1911.
Text: Eugene Field.
Agree: Agreement June 23, 1911: Gilchrist gave plates to Presser as cus-
todian to produce copies as demand required; royalty of 15 percent.
(Presser Documents.)
Price: $.40.
Royalty rate: $.06 per copy.
Royalties: September 1915, $12.60; September 1917, 1.44; September 1918,
1.56; September 1919, 1.14; 1920, 1.08; September 1921, 2.58; September
1922, 2.58; September 1923, 1.80; September 1924, 20 copies sold, 1.20;
September 1925, 1.04; September 1927, 1.56; September 1928, .60; Septem-
ber 1929, .84; September 1931, 1.40; September 1932, .80; September 1935,
.60; 1936, .60; 1937, .40.
Perf: Matinee Musical Club, March 31, 1914; MMS, November 29, 1916.
Copy: DLC.

ARRANGEMENTS

456. Adam, Adolphe. "O Holy Night."

Pub: Boston: Oliver Ditson Co., 1898.
Parts: Choral arrangement by W.W. Gilchrist, orchestrated by A.M. Kanrich.
Copy inf: Copyright renewed 1934.
Misc: ARG ledger notation, "Ditson finds no record of it, yet in 1935 he sold 763 copies of it, for which I got $6.10, started selling in 1928."

457. Brahms, Johannes. "Sandman, The."

Pub: Boston: Birchard and Co., 1906.

458. Fauré, Gabriel. "Santa Maria."

Misc: Title listed on "Hunting Song," published by G. Schirmer, New York.
Perf: MC, December 14, 1911.

459. Foster, Stephen C. "Old Black Joe."

Pub: Boston: Birchard and Co., 1906.

460. Franz, Robert. "Come Gracious Spirit."

Perf: MMS, May 19, 1915.

461. Gilchrist, William Wallace. Symphony in C major.

MS: Holograph in collection of PP.
Parts: Arrangement of Symphony for piano, four hands.

462. Gounod, Charles. "Nazareth."

182 William Wallace Gilchrist

MS: MS score and orchestra parts by copyist in collection of PP.
Parts: Violin I, 8 parts; violin II, 8 parts; viola, 5 parts; violoncello, 6 parts; bass, 3 parts; 1 part each: flute I, II; oboe, I, II; clarinet, I, II; bassoon I, II; horns, I, II, III, IV; trombones I, II, III, IV; bass trombone and tuba; tympani.
Copy inf: Copyright renewed 1921.
Misc: ARG listing, four hand arrangement with Schirmer, New York, 1897.
Agree: Assigned to Oliver Ditson, October 11, 1923. (Presser Documents.)
Perf: MC thirty-fifth anniversary concert, April 28, 1910, sung by MC, Treble Clef and Orpheus Club; Testimonial Concert to William Wallace Gilchrist, May 21, 1914; ARG ledger notation: taken out December 1923 for Strawbridge and Clothier, returned January 2, 1929.

463. Gounod, Charles. "Ring Out Wild Bells."

MS: Autograph in collection of PP.
Parts: SATB and orchestra (flute; oboe; clarinet; bassoon; horns I, II, III, IV; trumpet I, II; trombone; tuba; bells, tympani C, G, Bb; violin; viola; violoncello; bass).
Pub: Boston: Oliver Ditson Co., 1894.
Parts: SATB with piano.
Copy inf: Copyright renewed 1924.
Misc: Note on score, four hand accompaniment published separately.
Agree: Assigned to Oliver Ditson for $25 [no date]. (Presser Documents.)
Copy: CNJ.

464. Kulling, F.A. "Ah! Twinkling Star."

Pub: Boston: Oliver Ditson Co., 1913.
Parts: Women, three parts.
Text: C. Everest.
Price: $.10.
Royalty rate: 10 percent.
Perf: Oratorio Society of Philadelphia, February 16, 1903.

465. Shore, William. "Wavertree."

Pub: Presbyterian Hymnal. Philadelphia: Presbyterian Board of Public and Sabbath School Work, 1895.
Parts: Harmonized by W.W. Gilchrist.
Text: Two sets of words: Gerald Massey ("Surrounded by unnumbered foes"); Johann Scheffler ("Thee will I love, My Strength my Tower").

466.   Verdi, Guiseppi.   "Holy, Holy (Sanctus)," from <u>Requiem</u>.

<u>Parts</u>:   Condensed arrangement by W.W. Gilchrist.
<u>Copy inf</u>:   Entered in Catalog of Copyright Entries, April 1, 1903.

COLLECTIONS (CHILDREN)

467. Songs for the Children[7]

Pub: Philadelphia: Theodore Presser, 1897.
Agree: Agreements, royalty statements and receipts: December 31, 1896,
retail price $1.00, price to Presser, .40, Presser kept 104 copies at .40
each to cover cost of publishing, 41.54; February 1897, edition printed
from original plates with addition of "Fiddle-dee-dee," "Fairy and Child,"
"Mother's Song," "Three Little Kittens"; March 1, 1897, royalty, 500
copies, 119.47; royalty January 4, 1898, 40.00; January 17, 1898 receipt
from W.W. Gilchrist for 70 copies; royalty June 1898, 40.00: October 13,
1898, edition printed with addition of "March"; March 1899, edition printed
with addition of "Broken Doll," "Dinkey Bird," "Gingham Dog and Calico
Cat," "Sick Bird"; March 1899, royalty, 500 copies, 200.00; receipt from
W.W. Gilchrist for 381 copies, 500 printed at cost of 47.60, Presser kept
119 at .40 each to cover cost. (Presser Documents.)
Royalties: October 1918, $40.00; April 1925, 40.00.
Copy: Griffin collection, Cty.

---

[7]Songs listed in catalog individually by title.

COLLECTIONS (HYMNS)

468. Book of Common Praise (Hymnal Companion to the Prayer Book).

Pub: Philadelphia: Reformed Episcopal Publication Society, 1885. Compiled by James A. Moore, harmonies revised by W.W. Gilchrist.
Copy: PP.

469. Hymnal for use in Congregational Churches, The

Pub: Boston: Pilgrim Press, 1902. Edited by Louis F. Benson and William W. Gilchrist.
Copy: DLC.

470. Hymnal, The. Published by Authority of the General Assembly of the Presbyterian Church in the United States of America

Pub: Philadelphia: Presbyterian Board of Public and Sabbath School Work, 1895. William Wallace Gilchrist, musical editor.
Copy: DLC, NN.

471. Twelve Hymns Set to Music

Misc: Entered in Catalog of Copyright Entries, December 1, 1881.

COLLECTIONS (READERS)[8]

472. Educational Music Course

Pub: Boston: Ginn and Co., 1904, by James M. McLaughlin and W.W. Gilchrist.
Misc: Includes rote songs, voice training exercises, New First Music Reader, songs by famous composers.
Copy: DLC, KU, MB, MH, NNUT, OrU, Or, PU, RPB.

473. Educational Music Course, New

Pub: Boston: Ginn and Co., c. 1905-6, by J.M. McLaughlin, G.A. Veazie and W.W. Gilchrist.
Misc: 1st-[5th] reader.
Copy: Or, WaWW.

474. Educational Music Course, New

Pub: Boston: Ginn and Co., 1906, by James M. McLaughlin, George A. Veazie and W.W. Gilchrist.
Misc: Five volumes, songs with music, singing instruction books.
Copy: CoU, MB, MH, OrPR, OrP.

475. Educational Music Course, New

Pub: Boston: Ginn and Co., c. 1906-14, by James M. McLaughlin, George A. Veazie and W.W. Gilchrist.
Misc: Six volumes.
Copy: IU.

476. Educational Music Course, New

Pub: Boston: Ginn and Co., 1904, by James Matthew McLaughlin and William Wallace Gilchrist.
Misc: Teachers' edition for elementary grades, including a collection of rote songs, voice training exercises, First Music Reader, and songs from famous composers.
Copy: KU, MB, MH, NcD, OCl, OOxM, OU, WaWW.

---

[8]Arranged by level.

477. First Music Reader, New

Pub: Boston: Ginn and Co., 1903, by James M. McLaughlin, George A.
Veazie and W.W. Gilchrist.
Misc: School song book.
Copy: DLC, OO.

478. First [-second] Music Reader, New

Pub: Boston: Ginn and Co., c. 1903-4, by James Matthew McLaughlin,
G.A. Veazie and W.W. Gilchrist.
Copy: Or.

479. First Music Reader

Pub: Boston: Ginn and Co., 1906, by James M. McLaughlin, George A.
Veazie and W.W. Gilchrist.
Misc: School song book.
Copy: DLC, NcD, NN, OCT, OO, OEac, OOxM, PU, ViU.

480. Second Music Reader, New

Pub: Boston: Ginn and Co., 1904, by James M. McLaughlin and W.W.
Gilchrist.
Misc: School song book.
Copy: NN, OO.

481. Second Music Reader

Pub: Boston: Ginn and Co., 1906, by James M. McLaughlin and W.W.
Gilchrist.
Misc: School song book.
Copy: NN, ODW, OEac, OOxM, OU, PPT.

482. Third Music Reader

Pub: Boston: Ginn and Co., 1906, by James M. McLaughlin and W.W.
Gilchrist.
Misc: School song book.
Copy: DLC, NN.

483. Fourth Music Reader

Pub: Boston: Ginn and Co., 1905, 1906, by James M. McLaughlin and
W.W. Gilchrist.
Misc: School song book.
Copy: DLC, CU, NN, PU

484. Fourth Music Reader for Upper Grammar Classes and High Schools,
Advanced

Pub: Boston, 1895, by James Matthew McLaughlin and G.A. Veazie.
Misc: Two-part and three-part studies composed expressly for this work
by W.W. Gilchrist.
Copy: IU, OO.

485. Fifth Music Reader

Pub: Boston: Ginn and Co., 1906, by James M. McLaughlin and W.W.
Gilchrist.
Misc: School song book.
Copy: DLC, KMK, NN, OCT, OOxM, OU, PPT, RPB.

486. Song Reader

Pub: Boston: Ginn and Co., 1910, by James M. McLaughlin and W.W.
Gilchrist.
Misc: A graded course in school music in one book based on the New Edu-
cational Music Course.
Price: $.45.
Copy: MB, OrP, OU, Or, WaWW.

487. High School Music Reader

Misc: ARG listing, Ginn and Co., Boston, 1901. ARG ledger, "Purchased
... January 2, 1915 for $125."

488. Advanced Reader

Pub: Boston: Ginn and Co., 1902, by Luther W. Mason and W.W. Gilchrist, editors.
Copy: DLC.

COLLECTIONS (VOCAL EXERCISES)

489. Fundamental Exercises for the Voice

Pub: Philadelphia: Theodore Presser, 1912. Arranged and graded by
W.W. Gilchrist.
Agree: Agreement with Theodore Presser, December 23, 1911, copies sold
in advance exempt from royalty. (Presser Documents.)
Price: $.40.
Royalty rate: 6 percent.
Royalties: October 1913, $7.44; October 1914, 2.46; April 1915, 2.16; Oc-
tober 1915, 1.02; October 1916, 2.22; October 1917, 1.38; October 1918,
2.22; April 1919, 4.26; October 1919, 1.50; April 1921, .48; April 1923,
.36; October 1923, 1.50; April 1925, .12; October 1925, .30; May 1926,
.30; October 1926, .66; April 1928, 1.50.

490. Sight Singing Exercises, Book I

Pub: Philadelphia: Theodore Presser, 1892.
Agree: Agreements, royalty statements and receipts: December 1, 1892,
Presser had exclusive sale rights for two years, Presser advertised, Gilchrist sold to Presser in lots not less than 100 copies, cost $.22 each copy;
January 14, 1898, royalty $20.00; January 17, 1898 receipt from W.W. Gil-
christ for 398 copies; June 1898, royalty 29.04; August 1899, 300 copies
books I, II, III combined, royalty 113.29; October 17, 1899, royalty 50.00;
October 17, 1899, receipt from W.W. Gilchrist for 50 copies; November
1901, 500 printed at cost of 53.28, Presser kept 197 at .22 each to cover
cost; May 1906, 500 copies printed at cost of 47.92, Presser kept 218 at
.22 to cover cost; February 12, 1921, agreement between Anna R. Gilchrist
and Presser for continuation of publication and sale; 21 May, 290 copies
printed at cost of 27.25, Presser kept 153 at .22 each to cover cost; 500
copies printed at cost of 48.44, Presser kept 220 copies at .22 each to
cover cost. (Ibid.)
Royalty rate: $.22 per copy.
Royalties: April 1917, $22.00; February 1917, 22.00; October 1919, 22.00;
October 1920, new agreement, royalty per copy .10; royalties: April 1921,
34.60; October 1921, 17.90; April 1922, 7.60; October 1922, 12.10; April
1923, 8.00; October 1923, 15.00; April 1924, 11.30; October 1924, 23.10;
April 1925, 2.40; October 1925, 21.30; May 1926, 6.20; October 1926, 13.00;
April 1927, 10.50; November 1927, 14.40; April 1928, 8.80; October 1928,
5.60; April 1929, 17.70; October 1929, 19.80; April 1930, 4.70; October
1930, 6.40; April 1938–September 1938, 35 copies sold, 3.50.

491. Sight Singing Exercises, Book II

Pub: Philadelphia: Theodore Presser, 1892.

Agree: Agreements, royalty statements and receipts: December 1, 1892, Presser had exclusive sale rights for two years, Presser advertised, Gilchrist sold to Presser in lots not less than 100 copies, cost .20 each copy; January 14, 1898, royalty $13.20; January 17, 1898, receipt from W.W. Gilchrist for 188 copies; June 1898, royalty 13.20; August 1899, 300 copies book I, II, III combined, royalty 113.29; October 17, 1899, royalty 29.70; October 17, 1899, receipt from W.W. Gilchrist for 165 copies; February 17, 1902, 500 copies printed at cost of 40.85, Presser kept 205 at .20 each to cover cost; February 12, 1921, agreement between Anna R. Gilchrist and Presser for continuation of publication and sale; 500 copies printed at cost of 33.27, Presser kept 167 at .20 each to cover cost. (Presser Documents.)
Royalties: October 1919, $20; April 1920, new agreement, royalty per copy .10; royalties: October 1921, 20.00; October 1923, 6.60; April 1924, 21.60; October 1924, 8.20; April 1925, 1.30; October 1925, 8.90; May 1926, 7.30; October 1926, 1.60; April 1927, 7.10; October 1928, 3.40; April 1929, 9.90; October 1929, 5.70; April 1930, 8.70; October 1930, 6.40.

492.   Sight Singing Exercises, Book III

Pub: Philadelphia: Theodore Presser, 1892.
Misc: ARG ledger, April 1917, 100 copies from stock for Schirmer at $.40 each, $40.00.
Agree: Agreements, royalty statements and receipts: December 1, 1892, Presser had exclusive sale rights for two years, Presser advertised, Gilchrist sold to Presser in lots not less than 100 copies, cost .40 each copy; January 14, 1898, royalty 29.20; January 17, 1898, receipt from W.W. Gilchrist for 135 copies; June 1898, royalty 22.00; August 1899, 300 copies books I, II, III combined, royalty 113.29; October 17, 1899, royalty 33.60; October 17, 1899, receipt from W.W. Gilchrist for 216 copies; November 8, 1901, 300 copies printed at cost of 57.84, Presser kept 145 at .40 each to cover cost; February 12, 1921, agreement between Anna R. Gilchrist and Presser for continuation of publication and sale. (Ibid.)
Royalties: October 1917, $14.65; April 1920, new agreement, royalty per copy .20; royalties: October 1924, 9.20; April 1925, 6.40; October 1925, 10.40; May 1926, 5.40; October 1926, 13.20; April 1927, 3.40; November 1927, 3.00; April 1928, 6.00; October 1928, 2.20; April 1929, 4.40; October 1929, 3.20; April 1930, 3.20; October 1930, 4.20; April 1938-September 1938, seven copies sold, 1.40.

493.   [Three Hundred and thirty] 330 Exercises for Sight Singing Classes

Pub: Philadelphia: W.W. Gilchrist, c. 1891.
Copy: MiU, OO, OCT, PP. (This book is listed in the National Union Catalog, but is not in the catalog of the library at this time and was not found in the music department.)

INDEX OF FIRST LINES

Number refers to entry number in the catalog.

A bumble bee yellow as gold, 339
A little bird flew o'er the lea, 241
A widow bird sat mourning for her love, 451
A wind came up out of the sea, 268
Again the zephyrs take their flight, 192
All hail to thee fair morning, 351
All my heart this day rejoices, 235
All people that on earth do dwell, 145
All service ranks the same with God, 236
All the dear birdies are with us again, 420
All things so bright and beautiful, 33
And I saw the holy city, 350
Angels from the realms of glory, 238
Angels roll the stone away, 34
Arise my soul fly up and run, 55
Art thou hale for weariness, 435
As waves of pleasant sound, 219

Bedtimes come fo' little boys, 419
Behold my Servant whom I uphold, 38
Behold now fear ye not, 39
Behold! the days come saith the Lord, 62
Beneath the waning moon I walk at night, 208
Bird of the wilderness, 408
Bless the Lord O my soul, 45
Blessed morning, Blessed morning, 244
Blessed night when first that plain, 46
Blow on the mighty wind ("Hopkins"), 93
Blow on the mighty wind ("Whitsuntide"), 188
Branches are wailing, The, 329
Brightest and best of the sons of the morning, 247, 248
Busy is the carpenter, 253

Calm on the list'ning ear of night, 50
Children can you truly tell, 255
Christ is born the angels say, 256
Christ is risen from the dead, 56
Christ our Passover is sacrificed for us, 57, 58, 59
Christ the Lord is risen again, 60

Come o'er the sea, Maiden, with me, 242
Come see the place where Jesus lay (choral), 65
Come see the place where Jesus lay (song), 260
Come shout, come sing of the great sea king, 198

Daisies in the meadow, 370
Day is gently sinking to a close, The, 68
Day is past and over, The, 69
Day is quenched and the sun is fled, The, 415
Day of Resurrection, 267
Day will return with a fresher boon, 415
Days are cold, The, 263
Day's last ray disappears, 353
Dear Father always near us, 239
Dear frightened summer, 292
Dominus regit me, 72
Down the ages from afar, 274
Dream baby dream, 275
Dreaming forever vainly dreaming (choral), 200
Dreaming forever vainly dreaming (song), 276

Except the Lord build the house, 75

Fair stand the hills of Tennessee, 300
False fleeting youth, 207
Father hear the prayer we offer, 162
Father of all to Thee with loving hearts, we pray ("Father of All"), 76
Father of all to Thee with loving hearts we pray ("Way of Peace"), 183
Fill the bumper fair, 201
First a seed so tiny, 285
Flow down cold rivulet, 284
Flow'rs that my garden delighted, 386
Fly little bird in golden sun, 286
For the beauty of the earth, 159
Forsake me not!, 78
From far away we come to you, 288
From heav'n above the earth I come, 289
From North to South the anthem ring, 387
From the holy heaven, 80

Gingham dog and the calico cat, The, 290
Give ear O shepherd of Israel, 142
Glory be to the Lord, 82
Go fetch to me a pint o' wine, 413
Go to dark Gethsemene, 115
God is my strong salvation, 85
God is our refuge and strength, 79
God is our strength and refuge, 66
God of our Fathers (choral), 143

God of our Fathers (song), 384
God that madest earth and heaven, 86
God that madest earth and heaven ("Upsal"), 180
Good Christian people all, 294

Hail to the Lord's annointed, 87
Hark what mean those holy voices, 88
Hast thou a song, 295
He has come the Christ of God, 81
Hear O shepherd of Israel, 296
Hear the sledges with the bells, 193
Heav'n and earth rejoice, 298
Heavenly Father, breath thy blessing, 189
Hence! with all sorrow and tears, 315
Here awa', there awa', 299
Here upon my noble steed, 301
Here's a pretty cradle nest, 243
Hide me O twilight air, 437
Holy, Holy, Holy, 147
Home from the land of the summer and sun, 393
Home they brought her warrior dead, 204
Hosanna, loud hosanna, 94
How delicious is the winning of a kiss, 332
How glorious on the mountains, 125
How long wilt Thou forget me, 95
How many thoughts, 303
Hush my baby, 239

I beheld the earth, 61
I dream of thee at morn, 402
I dreamed of a cloudless heaven, 277
I gaed a waefu' gate yestreen, 245
I heard the voice of Jesus say, 96
I know a maid, 305
I know of a baby, 401
I know three little sisters, 283
I love Thee Lord, 98
I will lift up my eyes, 99
If life for me both joy or light, 234
If ye then be ris'n with Christ, 100
In an ocean way out yonder, 271
In her garden cool and shady, 346
In his tower sat the poet, 220
In love, if love be love, 307
In shoals and bands a novice train, 265
In the beginning was the word (choral), 100
In the beginning was the word (song), 308
In the gray of the gloaming, 269
In the hush of the Autumn night, 441
In the snowing and the blowing, 309
Inspirer and Hearer of prayer, 48
Into the sunshine full of the light, 287
Into the tomb of ages, past, 311

Is this thy promised fond regard, 251
It came upon a midnight clear (choral), 102, 103, 181
It came upon a midnight clear (song), 312
I've a message, 313

Jesus I my cross have taken, 104
Jesus lover of my soul, 105
Jesus, the very thought of Thee, 107
Joy fills the inmost heart today, 74
Just as I am, 113

King Death was a rare old fellow, 316
Knight, a sister's fond affection, 209

Late, late, so late!, 318
Lift up your hearts, 175
Lift your glad voices, 322
Light of light enlighten me, 323
Light of my darkness, 297
Light of the world we hail Thee, 117
Like as a Father pitieth his own children, 118
Little boy blue come blow your horn, 324
Little children can you tell, 54
Long shadows tell of days declining, 373
Long wears the day, 327
Lord have mercy upon me, 114
Lord Jesus come!, 67
Lord of little children, 443
Lord! Lord! Thou hast been our dwelling place, 126
Lord, what is man, 120
Lord with glowing heart I'd praise Thee, 91
Love calls in many tones, 412
Love me if I live, 331
Love thee dearest, love thee?, 262
Loving Saviour, Friend so dear, 333

Many a weary march and long, 371
Merry Christmas bells are ringing, 340
Mourn O rejoicing heart!, 434
My dolly broke her head today, 249
My heart is sair, 344
My heart to the heavens uprising, 422
My sins! my sins! my sins, 347
My soul doth magnify the Lord, 123
My soul in sorrow languishes, 293
My soul is dark, 348

Nae gentle dames, 345
No clouds are in the morning sky, 205
No, no it is not dying, 182
No, not despairingly, 128
No restful sleep mine eyelids know, 233
Now is my heart with weary waiting, 233
Now rest, ye pilgrim host, 129, 140
Now rosy May comes in wi' flow'rs, 264
Now therefore, ye that walk in darkness, 62
Now to heav'n our pray'r ascending, 130

(See also "Oh")
O blue eyes close in slumber, 409
O bread to pilgrims given, 77, 133
O Captain! my Captain! our fearful voyage done, 216
O Christmastide! O Christmastide!, 134
O God unseen yet ever near, 35
O heav'n born gift of song, 231
O Jesu, Thou art standing, 132
O Listen little Dear, 280
O little town of Bethlehem ("Bethlehem"--choral sacred), 44
O little town of Bethlehem, 135
O little town of Bethlehem (St. Louis Christmas), 146
O little town of Bethlehem (song), 356
O look at the moon, 357
O Lord the proud are risen, 136
O Lord Thou hast searched me out, 358
O many and many a year ago, 359
O mother my love, 254
O my laddie's gone away, 363
O my luve's like the red, red rose, 360
O praise Him, O praise Him, 116
O Saviour precious Saviour, 138
O star of Bethlehem!, 361
O the beauty and the glory!, 257
O the bonnie sailor boy, 246
O wonders amazing! At earth's midnight hour ("Easter Idyl"), 73
O wonder amazing! At earth's midnight hour ("Sewell"), 151
O'er the hill and o'er the dale, 362
Oft when storms of pain are rolling, 106
(See also "O")
Oh! Wert thou in the cauld blast, 365
Oh! Wert thou in the cauld, cauld blast, 364
Old mother Hubbard, 366
On the mountain top appearing, 367
Once in royal David's city, 368
Once there was a little voice, 369
One sweetly solemn thought, 53
One, two, three, four, march a-round, 337
Our Father makes each pretty cloud, 417
Out of the deep have I cried unto Thee, 70
Over our heads on the roof of the sky, 424
Over the river on the hill, 438

Passing out of the shadow into a pure light, 374
Peek-a-boo, peek-a-boo light, 326
Piping down the valley wild, 376
Ponder my words, 141
Poor little dicky bird drooping again, 405
Poor love, said life, that hast no gold, 319
Poor wounded heart farewell!, 379
Prayers of love like raindrops fell, 380
Pretty robin at my window welcoming the day, 273

Ring out wild bells (arrangement), 463
Ring out wild bells (song), 391
Rippling, purling little river, 392
Rise--Sleep no more, 304
Rock-a-bye baby on the treetop, 394
Rock-a-bye lady from hush-a-bye street, The, 395
Roseate hues of early dawn, The, 397
Row gently here my gondolier, 398

Sadly I wander'd, lonely my lot, 343
Sail fast, sail fast, sail fast, sail fast!, 203
Savior whom I fain would love, 150
Saviour like a shepherd lead us, 153
Sea is lonely, the sea is dreary, The, 229
Sea! the sea! the open sea! The, 399
See the lilies, how they grow, 400
Shadows of the evening hours, The, 152
She is a winsome wee thing, 403
Shine! Shine! Shine!, 223
Silent and soft from a measureless circle, 179
Sing, "Peace on earth, good will to men," 375
Sing! Sing! music was given to brighten the gay, 407
Sinners turn, why will ye die?, 158
Soft the daylight is declining, 349
Softly the echoes come and go, 411
Softly the summer air with balmy odors laden, 335
Something I may not win allures me, 414
Soul be quiet!, 382
Sound over all waters, 418
Splendor falls on castle walls, The (choral), 175
Splendor falls on castle walls, The (song), 250
Stop! Stop, pretty water, 425
Sun is ris'n and shall not set, The, 214
Sun who smiles wherever he goes, The, 427
Surrounded by unnumbered foes, 465
Sweet is true love tho' giv'n in vain, 428
Sweet saviour, bless us e're we go, 163

There once was a bird that lived up in a tree, 282
There was heard the sound of a coming foe, 210
There's a song in the air, 177

There's a twinkling little star, 423
This is the way the snow comes down, 410
Thou'rt like unto a flower, 432
Three little Kittens, they lost their Mittens, 433
Thus for the Lord hath led me on, 161
To Him who for our sins was slain, 157
To Jesus Christ the Lord, 178
To the northward point, 372
Turn fortune turn thy wheel, 436
'Twas in a forest absorb'd in thought, 452
'Twas on a Christmas morning, 258
Two hands upon the breast and labors done, 354
Two willing hands for work have I, 341

Unto light, unto life!, 279
Up to me sweet childhood looketh, 342

Wae! wae is my heart and the tear's in my e'e, 442
Waves of the far away ocean, 444
We are born, we laugh, we weep, 320
We lift them up to the Lord, 176
We praise Thee O Lord (C major), 173
We praise Thee O Lord (F major), 174
Weary of earth and laden with my sin, 184
Weep Mother Nature, weep!, 272
Welcome delightful morn, 36
What e'er my God ordains is right, 185
What is more gentle than a breeze in summer ("Sleep and Poetry"), 225
What is more gentle than a breeze in summer, 232
When first thy winning gaze I found, 429
When hope had fled and love seem'd dead, 330
When mother takes the fairy book, 281
When Spring comes tripping o'er the lea, 270
When the weary seeking rest, 186
When thou art nigh it seems a new creation round, 445
When twilight dews are falling fast, 446
Where bloom celestial roses, 187
Where e'er I wander, far or near, 447
Where would I be at morn!, 448
While shepherds watched their flocks by night, 449
Why shines the moon so dim tonight?, 450
Wind is rustling thro' the covers, The, 206
Winter days have vanished, The, 240
Wise men once beheld a star, The, 381
With bitter grief my heart is aching, 453
With songs and honors sounding loud, 40
Woodman cuts the forest tree, The, 454
Wynken, and Blynken and Nod one night, 455

SOURCES CONSULTED

Books

Burt, Nathaniel. The Perennial Philadelphians: The Anatomy of an Amer-
    ican Aristocracy. Boston: Little, Brown & Co., 1963; reprint ed.,
    Salem, N.Y.: Ayer Co., 1975.
Campbell, Jane. Old Philadelphia Music. Philadelphia: City History Soci-
    ety, 1926.
Carson, Hampton Lawrence, ed. History of the Celebration of the One
    Hundredth Anniversary of the Promulgation of the Constitution of the
    United States. 2 vols. Philadelphia: J.B. Lippincott, 1889.
Chase, Gilbert. America's Music, from the Pilgrims to the Present. New
    York: McGraw-Hill Book Co., 1955; 2nd rev. ed., 1966; reprint ed.,
    Westport, CT.: Greenwood Press, 1981.
Cheyney, Edward Potts. History of the University of Pennsylvania, 1740-
    1940. Philadelphia: University of Pennsylvania Press, 1940.
Collins, William F. Laurel Winners: Portraits and Silhouettes of Modern
    Composers. Cincinnati: John Church Co., 1900.
Ellinwood, Leonard. The History of American Church Music. New York:
    Morehouse-Gorham Co., 1953; reprint ed., New York: Da Capo, 1970.
Elson, Louis C. The History of American Music. New York: Macmillan
    Co., 1915; reprint ed., New York: B. Franklin, 1971.
Gerson, Robert A. Music in Philadelphia. Philadelphia: Theodore Presser
    Co., 1940; reprint ed., Westport, CT.: Greenwood Press, [1976].
Gilchrist, William Wallace. Journal and Poetry. Unpublished bound volume.
Goepp, Philip Henry. Symphonies and Their Meaning. Philadelphia: J.B.
    Lippincott Co., 1902.
Goodrich, A.J. Complete Musical Analysis. Cincinnati: John Church Co.,
    1889.
Howard, John Tasker. Our American Music. 4th ed. New York: Thomas
    Y. Crowell Co., 1965.
Hughes, Rupert. Contemporary American Composers. Boston: L.C. Page
    & Co., 1900.
Rohrer, Gertrude Martin. Music and Musicians of Pennsylvania. Philadel-
    phia: Theodore Presser Co., 1940; reprint ed., [Port Washington,
    N.Y.]: Friedman, 1970.
Smith, William James, ed. Granger's Index to Poetry. 6th ed. New York:
    Columbia University Press, 1973.
Upton, William Treat. Art Song in America. Boston: Oliver Ditson Co.,
    1930.
Wister, Frances A. Twenty-Five Years of the Philadelphia Orchestra, 1900-
    1925. Philadelphia: Edward Stern & Co., 1925; reprint ed., Salem,
    N.Y.: Ayer Co., [1970].

Collections

Children

Gilchrist, William Wallace. Songs for the Children. Philadelphia: Theodore
    Presser, 1897.

Children

Gilchrist, William Wallace. Songs for the Children. Philadelphia: Theodore
    Presser, 1897.

Hymns

Benson, Louis F. and Gilchrist, William W., eds. The Hymnal for use in
    Congregational Churches. Boston: Pilgrim Press, 1902.
Book of Worship. New York: New Church Board of Publication, 1950, 1960,
    1968, 1982.
First Songs for Little Children. Ann Arbor: Edwards Brothers, 1957.
Gilchrist, William Wallace, ed. The Hymnal. Published by the Authority
    of the General Assembly of the Presbyterian Church in the United States
    of America. Philadelphia: Presbyterian Board of Public and Sabbath
    School Work, 1895.
Hosanna, The. New York: New Church Press, 1920, 1932.
Hosanna, The. revised ed. Boston: The Swedenborg Press, 1968.
Hosanna for Children. New York: New Church Board of Publication, 1888,
    1905.
Hymnal for Schools and Families. Ann Arbor: Edwards Brothers, 1914,
    1964 editions.
Liturgy for the General Church of the New Jerusalem, A. Bryn Athyn,
    Pa.: Academy Book Room, 1908, 1916, 1921, 1939, 1966 editions.
Magnificat, The. New York: New Church Board of Publication, 1893, 1910,
    1911.
Moore, James A., comp., Gilchrist, W.W., reviser of harmonies. Book of
    Common Praise (Hymnal Companion to the Prayer Book). Philadelphia:
    Reformed Episcopal Publication Society, 1885.
New Hosanna, The. New York: New Church Board of Publication, 1902.

Readers   (Arranged by level)

McLaughlin, James M. and Gilchrist, W.W. Educational Music Course.
    Boston: Ginn & Co., 1904.
McLaughlin, James M., Veazie, George A., and Gilchrist, W.W. New First
    Music Reader. Boston: Ginn & Co., 1903.
_____. First Music Reader. Boston: Ginn & Co., 1906.
McLaughlin, James M., and Gilchrist, W.W. Second Music Reader. Boston:
    Ginn & Co., 1904.
_____. New Second Music Reader. Boston: Ginn & Co., 1906.
_____. Third Music Reader. Boston: Ginn & Co., 1906.
_____. Fourth Music Reader. Boston: Ginn & Co., 1905.
_____. Fifth Music Reader. Boston: Ginn & Co., 1906.
_____. Song Reader. Boston: Ginn & Co., 1910.
_____. High School Music Reader. Boston: Ginn & Co., 1901.
Mason, Luther and Gilchrist, W.W. Advanced Reader. Boston: Ginn &
    Co., 1902.

Dictionaries, Encyclopedias and Directory

American History and Encyclopedia of Music, 1908 ed. S.v. "Gilchrist,
    William Wallace."
Dictionary of American Biography, 1932 ed. S.v. "Gilchrist, William Wal-
    lace," by F.H.M. [Frederick Herman Martins].
Encyclopedia of Associations. 2 vols Vol. 2: National Organizations of the
    United States, 1975 ed. S.v. "National Institute of Arts and Letters."
Grove's Dictionary of Music and Musicians, American Supplement, 1928 ed.;
    reprinted, with new material, 1935, 1952. S.v. "American College of

Musicians."
_____. "American Guild of Organists."
_____. "Gilchrist, William Wallace."
_____. "Music Teachers' National Association."
Handbook of American Music and Musicians, 1887 ed. S.v. "Gilchrist, William Wallace."
New Grove Dictionary of Music and Musicians, 1980 ed. S.v. "Gilchrist, William Wallace," by Robert Stevenson.
Philadelphia Bureau Of Music, comp. Musical Survey and Directory. Philadelphia, 1929.

Magazines and Journals

Authors Named

Gilchrist, William Wallace. "A Maid's Choice." Harper's Monthly 84 (December 1891): 16-26.
_____. "Philadelphia Singing Societies." Musical Courier 29 (December 1899): 33-34.
Goepp, Philip H. "The Musical Art Club of Philadelphia." Musician 18 (October 1913): 664.
Hall, Walter Henry. "W.W. Gilchrist. An Appreciation." New Music Review 16 (February 1917): 470-71.
Krehbiel, E.H. "American Choral Societies and Conductors." Harper's Weekly, February 1, 1890, pp. 95-96.
Maitland, Rollo F. "The Gilchrist Centenary." Crescendo 8 (January 1946): 3-4.
Sumner, Salter. "Early Encouragements to American Composers." The Musical Quarterly 18 (January 1932): 75-105.

No Authors Given

"Completion of the Unfinished Symphony." Art Alliance Bulletin, April 1937, p. 10.
"Dr. William Wallace Gilchrist." Etude 63 (December 1945): 661.
"Dr. William Wallace Gilchrist." New Church Messenger, March 7, 1917, p. 195.
"Home City to Observe Centenary of Birth of Dr. W.W. Gilchrist." Diapason 434 (January 1946): 14.
"Notes: A Testimonial." Musical Philadelphia, February 1917, p. 5.
"Philadelphia Commemorates Gilchrist Anniversary." New Church Messenger, February 2, 1946, p. 46.
"Second Concert of the Philadelphia Manuscript Music Society." Music, July 1894, pp. 315-16.
"W.W. Gilchrist." Etude 17 (May 1899): 136.
"William Wallace Gilchrist." The Helper 97 (February 1936): 1-2.

Newspapers

Newspapers are listed in alphabetical order, articles under each newspaper title are listed in chronological order.

Author Named

Philadelphia Item. Lawes, John H. "Gilchrist Honored." 12 May 1899. Included in Gilchrist scrapbook, p. 62.
Philadelphia Public Ledger. Goepp, Philip H. "William W. Gilchrist. A Timely Appreciation." 4 April 1915, sec. 2, p. 5.

_____. Ingham, John H. "Philadelphia Orchestra. History of Its Origin by One of the Prime Movers (letter to editor)." 8 February 1917, p. 10.

No Author Named

Boston Transcript. "Recent Deaths. Noted Composer and Organist." 21 December 1916, p. 16.

Cincinnati Commercial. "A Glorious Ending. The Feast of Song Closes Triumphantly." 20 May 1882. Included in Gilchrist scrapbook, p. 53.

Harrisburg Patriot. "Choral Society's Music Festival Greatest in the Organization's History." 24 April 1909. Included in Gilchrist scrapbook, p. 50.

Harrisburg Telegraph. "May Festival Concerts Are Well Received." 16 May 1908, p. 2.

_____. "W.W. Gilchrist." 21 December 1916, p. 9.

New York Times. "Gilchrist Testimonial." 12 May 1899. Included in Gilchrist scrapbook, p. 62.

Philadelphia Evening Bulletin. "The Mendelssohn Club to Extend Its Scope." [Ca. 1899]. Included in Gilchrist scrapbook, p. 158.

_____. "Mendelssohn Club Concert." April 1907. Included in Gilchrist scrapbook, p. 9.

Philadelphia Evening Bulletin. "Dr. W.W. Gilchrist, Composer, Is Dead." 20 December 1916, pp. 1-2.

_____. "Honor Late Dr. Gilchrist." 8 January 1946, p. 5.

Philadelphia Evening Telegraph. "Gilchrist Testimonial." 12 May 1899, p. 2.

Philadelphia Inquirer. "The Mendelssohn Club." 19 April 1907, p. 9.

_____. "William Wallace Gilchrist." 21 December 1916, p. 10.

Philadelphia Item. "Manuscript Music Society Concert." 21 November 1901, p. 7.

Philadelphia North American. "Mendelssohn Club." 17 January 1909, sec. 7, p. 6.

Philadelphia Press. "Gilchrist Testimonial." 12 May 1899, p. 9.

_____. "Dr. Gilchrist Symphony Played." 5 March 1910, p. 3.

_____. "Musical Art Club Plans Memorial to Dr. Gilchrist." 21 December 1916, p. 5.

Philadelphia Public Ledger. "Gilchrist Cantata Heard." 19 April 1907, p. 3.

_____. "Mendelssohn Season Opens." 24 January 1908, p. 3.

_____. "Musical Notes." 3 October 1909, sec. 2, p. 3.

_____. "Musical Notes." 27 February 1910, sec. 2, p. 8.

_____. "Manuscript Music Society." 20 March 1910, sec. 7, p. 10.

_____. "Manuscript Music Society, Twenty-Third Season." 26 February 1914, p. 9.

_____. "Dr. Gilchrist's Work." 28 March 1915. Included in Gilchrist scrapbook, p. 115.

Philadelphia Public Ledger. "Honoring a Great Philadelphian." 10 April 1915, p. 10.

_____. "The Works of Dr. Gilchrist." 15 April 1915. Included in Gilchrist scrapbook, p. 115.

_____. "William Wallace Gilchrist." 21 December 1916, p. 17.

_____. "Music and Musicians." 14 January 1917, p. 6.

Philadelphia Record. "This Fine New Club to Advance City's Musical Art." 2 May 1909, p. 2.

No Newspaper Named

"Musical Highlights of 25 Years Ago." April 1940. Included in Gilchrist scrapbook, p. 156.

Miscellaneous Materials

Announcements
Church Manual. Church of the New Jerusalem, January 1946.
Concerts and Recitals. Harrisburg Choral Society, 1895-1909.
Events at Church of the New Jerusalem, March and April 1909.
First Presbyterian Church, April 1925.
Gilchrist Testimonial, May 11, 1899.
Performance of "Lamb of God." Saint Paul's Chapel, Columbia University,
    March 21, 1917.
Prospectus and Announcements of the Mendelssohn Club of Philadelphia.
Walnut Street Presbyterian Church, April 1933.
William Wallace Gilchrist Memorial, February 19, 1917.

Catalogs
Dictionary Catalog of the Music Collection [of the] Boston Public Library.
    20 vols. Boston: G.R. Hall & Co., 1972.
Fleisher, Edwin A. The Edwin A. Fleisher Music Collection in the Free
    Library of Philadelphia. 2 vols. Philadelphia: Privately printed, 1933
    (vol. I); 1945 (vol. II).
National Union Catalog Pre-1956 Imprints. London: Mansell Information &
    Publishing, Ltd., 1969.
The Allen A. Brown Collection of Music. 4 vols. Boston: Boston Public
    Library, 1910-16.
United States Copyright Office. Catalog of Copyright Entries and Indexes.
    Washington: Copyright Office of the Library of Congress, 1870-1974.

Certificate of Death, Letters of Administration, Wills
Certificate of Death. William Wallace Gilchrist. Commonwealth of Pennsyl-
    vania, Department of Health. File No. 124245.
Letters of Administration for William Wallace Gilchrist, filed at City Hall,
    Philadelphia, Pa., #36-1917.
Will of Anna R. Gilchrist (May 29, 1871-May 30, 1953), filed at City Hall,
    Philadelphia, Pa., W#1725, 1953.
Will of Susan B. Gilchrist, filed at City Hall, Philadelphia, Pa. #2636-1931.
Constitution and By-Laws of the Manuscript Music Society. Philadelphia:
    George H. Buchanan & Co. [ca. 1891-92].

Correspondence
Burbank, Ellen to Martha Furman Schleifer.
Daboll, Mary to Martha Furman Schleifer.
Gilchrist Children to William Wallace Gilchrist.
Gilchrist, Redelia Cox to William Wallace Gilchrist.
Gilchrist, William to William Wallace Gilchrist.
Gilchrist, William Wallace to Gilchrist Children.
Gilchrist, William Wallace to Miscellaneous Persons.
Miscellaneous Persons to William Wallace Gilchrist.
In Memoriam Booklet. Tribute to William Wallace Gilchrist from Musical Fund
    Society, 1917.

Interviews
Gilchrist, Edmund Jr. with Martha Furman Schleifer, 1975-76.
Griffin, Margaret with Martha Furman Schleifer, 1971-72.

Programs

During and after Gilchrist's lifetime if no specific date is given assume
Philadelphia unless otherwise noted.

Cathedral of Saint John the Divine, Columbia University, New York, New
    York, April 1, 1909.
Church of the New Jerusalem.
Civic Symphony Orchestra, 1937–38.
Institute Hall, March 1, 1878.
"Jerusalem," April 24, 1890.
Manuscript Music Society.
Matinee Musical Club, March 31, 1914, February 3, 1925.
May Music Festival Programs 1883, 1884.
Melody Club, 1903–4.
Mendelssohn Club
Miscellaneous Programs in Gilchrist scrapbook and collections of Free Li-
    brary of Philadelphia and Pennsylvania Historical Society, 1860-to present.
Musical Alumni of the University of Pennsylvania, June 4, 1917.
Pennsylvania Day Program, August 30, 1926.
Pennsylvania Music Teachers Association Annual Convention and Music
    Festival, 1893, 1894.
Philadelphia Orchestra Programs 1901-to present and Index of Concerts and
    Programs, 1902–3.
Symphony Society, 1892–1900.
W.P.A. (Works Progress Administration) Composers' Forum Laboratory,
    May 21, 1937.

Photographs
Collections of Ellen Burbank and Gilchrist scrapbook.

Reports
Manuscript Music Society. Reports of the Secretary and Treasurer. Phila-
    delphia: Privately printed October 4, 1893; October 3, 1894.
    Reports of the Board of Direction. 1895-1896; October 19, 18989; 1909.
Music Teachers' National Association. Fifty Years of Music in America,
    1876-1926. Proceedings, 1928.
Pennsylvania State. Educational Monographs. A Presentation of Accom-
    plishments and Objectives in Education in Pennsylvania. Harrisburg,
    April 1926.
Philadelphia School District. Annual Report of the Superintendent of Pub-
    lic Schools, Philadelphia 1897. Philadelphia: Burk & McFetridge Co.,
    1898.

Scrapbooks
Gilchrist Family. Contains miscellaneous letters, magazine and newspaper
    articles, photographs and programs of the Gilchrist family, 1878-1946.
Zeckwer, Camille. I: Inscribed: "Camille Zeckwer, Pianist. The Tracy,
    36th and Chestnut, Philadelphia."
_____. II: Inscribed "1891."
_____. III: Inscribed "1903."
Zimmerman, Edward. Contains newspaper articles and programs, 1886-91.
Zimmerman, Marie Kunkel. I, II, III: newspaper articles and programs.

A'Becket, Thomas, Jr., 33, 45

Abt Male Singing Society (Philadelphia), 5

Academy of Music, 16, 28, 38

Allen A. Brown Collection, v

Amateur Drawing Room, 4

American College of Musicians, 9

American Guild of Organists, 19

Amphion Society of Germantown (Philadelphia), 8

"Andante in C" (for organ), 31

Arcadian (singing society, Philadelphia), 8

Art Alliance, 29

"Ave Maria," 41

Beaman, E.A. (Reverend), 4
  Polly, 23
  Susan (see also Susan B. Gilchrist), 1, 3, 4

Becker, John B., 40

Beddoe, Daniel, 37

"Behold now, Fear Ye Not," 31

Belgium, 12

"Bells, The," 50

Belmont Cricket Club, 12

"Blue Eyed Lassie," 24

Boner, William H., 5, 6, 33

Boston Festival Orchestra, 18, 19

Cathedral of Saint John the Divine (New York), 23

Central Music School, 18

"Charm Me Asleep," 50

"Cherry Ripe," 24, 31, 43

Choral Society of Philadelphia, 37, 38

Christ Church (Germantown, Philadelphia), vi, 5

"Christ the Lord is Risen Today," 54

"Christmas Idyll, A," 18, 55

Church Choral Society of Reading (Pennsylvania), 38

Church, John, Company, vii

Church of the New Jerusalem (Philadelphia), vi, 5, 23, 24, 25, 31, 47, 50

Cincinnati, Ohio, 5

Cincinnati (Ohio) Festival Association, 5

Cincinnati (Ohio) May Festival, 5

Civic Symphony Orchestra, 30

Civil War, 1

Clarke, Hugh, 3, 9, 45, 46
  James, 4

Cole, Lucius, 40

Columbia University, 23

Composers' Forum Laboratory, 30

Conservatory of Miss Bauer (Cincinnati), 5

Cox, Charles, 1, 3
  Redelia Ann (see also Redelia Gilchrist), 1, 3

Cross, Michael H., 45

"Dainty Davie," 29
"Day is Gently Sinking," 42,
    50
"De Profundis," 9
"Descant," 50
Ditson, Oliver, Company, vii
Douty, Nicholas, 42
"Dreaming," 5

"Easter Idyl," 22, 37, 55
Eurydice Chorus, 22
Evans, Edwin, 42

Fantasie for Violin and Piano,
    29, 30, 47, 49
"Fantasy for Organ," 47
First New Jerusalem Society
    (Cincinnati, Ohio), 5
First Presbyterian Church
    (Philadelphia), 23
Fleisher Collection, v, 21, 29
Fleisher Symphony Concert
    Orchestra, 30
"Forty-Sixth Psalm," vi, 6,
    52, 53, 55, 58
"Fountain, The," 24, 50
Free Library of Philadelphia,
    v, 21, 25, 29, 31
    Chamber Music Collection, v

Geneva, Switzerland, 14
Germania Orchestra, 7
Germantown Choral, 10
Germany, 12
Gilchrist, Anna, v, vi, vii,
    4, 17, 20, 23, 25, 26,
    29, 31, 43, 52, 54
    Charles, 4, 21
    Edmund, 4, 21, 26, 30
    James, 1
    Redelia, 1, 3
    Susan B., 14, 26
    Wallace, 4, 14, 21
    William, 1, 2, 3
Gilchrist, William Wallace

army experience, 1-3
centennial of birth, 30, 43
depression, 7, 8, 13, 14, 20,
    25, 51
marital problems, 15
memorials, 26-31, 50
music, discussion of, 51-57
prizes in composition, 5, 55
testimonial concerts, 6, 10,
    16, 19, 30, 33, 34, 40, 42,
    58
"Gingham Dog and the Calico
    Cat, The," 50, 52
Goepp, Philip, 45, 50, 53
"Gone Before," 51

Hahn, Frederic, 40
Hahn Quartette, 48, 49
Hall, Walter Henry, 23, 27
Handel and Haydn Society, 4
Happich, William, 29
Harmonia, 5
Harrisburg Choral Society, 5,
    18, 24
"Heart's Delight," 24, 29, 41,
    51, 52, 53
"Here Awa', There Awa'," 24,
    30, 41, 42, 50
Hille, Gustave, 46
Historical Society of Pennsyl-
    vania, v
Holy Trinity Episcopal Church
    (Philadelphia), 4
"How Many Thoughts," 30, 41
"Hunting Song," 56

"In Autumn," 5
"In the Blush of Evening," 41

Jarvis, Charles, 45
Jersey City, New Jersey, 1
John Hay Library at Brown Uni-
    versity, v
"Joys of Spring," 54

Keely Abbie R., 40
Knauss, Charles E., 41
Kneisel, Carl, 40
Kneisel Quartet of Boston, 16
"Knight of Toggenburg," 47

"Lamb of God," 23, 31, 55
Lang, Henry A., 46
Langston, Marie Stone, 42
"Legend of the Bended Bow,
    The," 18
Leman, J.W.F., 30, 40
Library of Congress, v
"Little John Bottle John," 50
London, England, 11, 12
Lucerne, Switzerland, 12
"Lullaby," 53

McClosky, Elizabeth I., 3
McCollin, Edward G., 44
    Frances, 50
Maclaughlin, Annie L., 36
"Maid's Choice, A," vi, 15
Manuscript Music Society, 15,
    24, 25, 30, 40, 44-50,
    58
    Constitution and By-Laws,
    44-45
    Report of the Secretary,
    1893, 46; 1894, 47
    Report of the Board of
    Direction, 1895-1896, 47;
    1898, 47; 1909, 48
Matinee Musical Club, 24, 29,
    50
Matthews, H. Alexander, 40
"Meadow Talk," 50
Melody Club (Philadelphia), 22
Melody Club (Woodbury, New
    Jersey), 24
Mendelssohn Club of New
    York, 5
Mendelssohn Club of Philadel-
    phia, vi, vii, 5, 10, 16,
    17, 19, 21, 22, 24, 25,
    30, 31, 32-43, 45, 58
    fiftieth anniversary, 42

Motto Song (see also, "Ode
    to Song"), 41, 43, 50
    orchestra, 33
Mendelssohn Festival, 38
Milione, Louis, 28
Mohr, Herman, 46
Music Teachers' National Associ-
    ation (M.T.N.A.), 9
Musical Art Club, 23, 24
Musical Fund Society, vi, 28
"My Highland Lassie, O," 52, 53
"My Ladye," 49
"My Sins, My Sins, My Saviour,"
    41

National Association of American
    Composers and Conductors,
    30
National Institute of Arts and
    Letters, 20
National Union Catalog, v
"Nature's Lullaby," 52, 53
"Nazareth" (Gounod-Gilchrist),
    37, 41
Nazareth, Pennsylvania, 14
"New Jerusalem, The," 52
New York Public Library at
    Lincoln Center, v
"Ninetieth Psalm," 25, 30, 42
Nonet, 31, 45, 47, 48, 49, 56
Norden, N. Lindsay, 42

"O Lord Thou Hast Searched
    Me Out," 31, 41, 53, 54
"Ode to Song (Mendelssohn
    Club Motto)," 41, 43, 50
"Ode to the Sun," 5
Orpheus Club, 22
"Our Country Friends," 52
Our Music Society (O.M.S.), 4
Oxford University, 4

Paris, France, 14
Pennsylvania State Music Teach-
    ers' Association, 18

Philadelphia Chorus, 8
Philadelphia Music Club, 24
Philadelphia Music Festival,
    7, 8
Philadelphia Musical Academy,
    6, 45
Philadelphia Orchestra, 4,
    17, 18, 22, 25, 28, 30,
    36, 42, 48, 59, 57
"Philadelphia Singing Societies"
    (article by W.W. Gil-
    christ), 16
Pohlig, Carl, 21
"Ponder My Words," 31
Presbyterian Church of the
    United States, 19
Presser, Theodore, Company,
    vii
Public Library of the City of
    Boston, v
Public School System of Phila-
    delphia, 20

Quinlan, Agnes Clune, 40
Quintette in C minor, number
    1, 15, 50
Quintette, in F major, number
    2, 24, 30, 31, 49

Reinecke, Carl, 5
"Ring Out, Wild Bells" (Gou-
    nod-Gilchrist), 33
"Rose, The," 41, 55

Saint Clement's Church (Phila-
    delphia), v, 5, 32
Saint Mark's Church (Phila-
    delphia), 4
Saint Thomas Church (Epis-
    copal, Fort Washington)
    25
Saint-Saëns, Camille, 5
Scheel, Fritz, 22, 36
Schirmer, G., Company, vii
Schmitz, Charles M., 7, 8

Schubert Choir of York (Penn-
    sylvania), 38
Scott, Henri G., 37
"Sea-Fairies, The," 32
Second Presbyterian Church
    (Philadelphia), 23, 31
Serenade, 24
Sesquicentennial Exposition, 22
"Sing! Sing!," 53
"Sirens, The," 24
"Song of Doubt, and a Song of
    Faith, A," 51-52, 53
Songs for the Children, vi
Stokowski, Leopold, 42, 49
Stone, Alonzo, 46
Suite for Violin and Piano, num-
    ber 1, 22
"Sweet is True Love," 49
"Sweetheart," 5
"Symphonic Poem," 25, 28, 30
Symphony Club, 29
Symphony in C major, number 1,
    18, 21, 30, 31, 46, 53, 56,
    57
Symphony in D major (second),
    29, 56
Symphony Society, 15, 16, 17,
    18, 21, 34, 58

Temple University, 29, 30
Thomas, Theodore, 5
"Thou'rt Like Unto a Flower,"
    41, 50
Tily, Herbert J., 40, 49
Trauble, Gertrude, 31
Trio in G minor (for Violin, Cel-
    lo and Piano), 10, 22, 47,
    49
Tuesday club of Wilmington Dela-
    ware, 5

Une Petite Suite, for piano,
    four hands, 46, 47
University of Pennsylvania, 4,
    18, 21, 24, 25, 28, 29, 40
"Uplifted Gates, The," 33, 41,
    42, 55

Upper Saranac Lake, New
    York, 7

"Voice of the Sea, The," 52

Wadlow, J. Harry, 40
Walnut Street Presbyterian
    Church (Philadelphia),
    23
Warner, Massah, 45
"Waves of the Far Away

Ocean," 52
West Philadelphia Choral Soci-
    ety, 5, 6, 8
Westminster Abbey, 11
"When Thou Art Nigh," 5
Works Progress Administration
    (W.P.A.), 30
"Wynken, Blynken and Nod,"
    24, 50

Zeckwer, Camille, 6, 46
Zimmerman, E.M., 37, 45
Zimmerman, Marie Kunkel, 42